31.45

-101-
TIPS
for Graduates

A Code of Conduct for Success and Happiness in Your Professional Life

SUSAN MOREM

Ferguson
An imprint of ☑®Facts On File

101 Tips for Graduates

Copyright © 2005 by Susan Morem

All rights reserved. No part of this book may be reproduced or utilized in any form or by any means, electronic or mechanical, including photocopying, recording, or by any information storage or retrieval systems, without permission in writing from the publisher. For information contact:

Ferguson
An imprint of Facts On File, Inc.
132 West 31st Street
New York NY 10001

Library of Congress Cataloging-in-Publication Data
Morem, Susan.
101 Tips for graduates: a code of conduct for success and happiness in your professional life / Susan Morem.
p. cm.
Includes index.
ISBN 0-8160-5676-5 (alk. paper)
1. Success in business. 2. Performance. 3. Employees—Attitudes. 4. Self-management (Psychology) 5. College graduates—Life skills guides. 6. Young adults—Life skills guides. I. Title: One hundred and one tips for graduates. II. Title: One hundred and one tips for graduates. III. Title.
HF5386.M754 2005
650.1—dc22   2004021601

Ferguson books are available at special discounts when purchased in bulk quantities for businesses, associations, institutions, or sales promotions. Please call our Special Sales Department in New York at (212) 967-8800 or (800) 322-8755.

You can find Ferguson on the World Wide Web at http://www.fergpubco.com

Text design by Mary Susan Ryan-Flynn

Printed in the United States of America

MP FOF 10 9 8 7 6 5 4 3 2 1

This book is printed on acid-free paper.

TABLE OF CONTENTS

COMMUNICATION SKILLS
Achieve Effective Communication Through Body Language, Listening, Speaking, and Writing

LEADERSHIP SKILLS
Become a Leader

SOCIAL SKILLS
Maintain Good Relationships and Work
Cooperatively with Others

SELF-DISCIPLINE
Be Healthy, Wealthy, and Wise

DEMONSTRATE A POSITIVE ATTITUDE
Make Your Life a Little Easier

AREAS OF DISTINCTION
Rise Above the Ordinary and
Live an Extraordinary Life

APPENDIX: EXTRA CREDIT BONUS INSIGHTS

INDEX

Acknowledgments

This book is the result of the contributions made by many people. To those of you who responded to my request for input, thank you for taking the time to respond and for sharing your personal stories and sage advice. Your contribution is appreciated more than you know.

Thank you, Melissa Abrams and Demae Derocher, for your creative input. Melissa, I value your honesty, your insight, and your objectivity. Thank you for sharing so many of your ingenious ideas with me. Demae, you are one of the most resourceful and determined people I know. Thank you for your diligence and commitment. I will miss the late night conversations, the detailed e-mails, and the insight I gained by spending time with you.

Thank you, Sharron Stockhausen, for your gentle guidance and keen insight. When I was overwhelmed, you calmed me. When I had doubts, you reassured me. You listened to me, you encouraged me, and you helped me accomplish what I set out to do.

Thank you, James Chambers, for enthusiastically embracing the concept of this book, for being receptive to the changes I made, and for supporting me through the challenges I faced as I was writing it. I can't imagine working with a better editor!

Writing two books simultaneously presented more challenges than I ever anticipated. I am fortunate to have understanding friends and a wonderful family who patiently waited for me to resurface after I placed our relationships on hold in order to meet my deadlines. A special thank you and acknowledgement goes to my husband, Steve, and to my daughters, Stephanie, Stacie, and Samantha, for giving me the space I needed, for cheering me on, and for loving me unconditionally. I am truly blessed to have each one of you in my life.

This book was written for and is dedicated to anyone who is transitioning from one stage of life to another, to all past, present, and future graduates, and to my three daughters who inspired me to write it.

Introduction

I've been fortunate to have the opportunity to speak with hundreds of high school and college students over the last few years, and every time I do, I am inspired. I have three daughters of my own—two in college and one in high school, and I've seen firsthand how competitive their world has become. Students must work hard to achieve academic success. They face fierce competition both in gaining admission into the college of their choice and in finding a job in their chosen profession.

Today, high school and college students live in a time of rapid change and enormous advancement. It is not uncommon for young adults to own a personal computer, automobile, television, cell phone, unlimited articles of clothing, and too many CDs to count. They have more disposable income than generations before, and although they enjoy many privileges, they also face some of life's darkest moments and harshest realities.

I am motivated by young adults because *they* are motivated. I see possibilities for them because *they* see possibilities. I am optimistic about their future because *they* are optimistic, at least for now. Unfortunately, as time passes, I've seen too many people replace optimism with pessimism and either limit or give up on themselves.

I don't ever want my daughters to give up on their dreams, and I don't want the bright and talented young adults who have inspired me to lose their inspiration. In an attempt to prevent new graduates from becoming a future generation of grumpy old men and women who age with regret, I decided to do something to help make their lives a little easier.

I wondered if I could find a way to help prepare young adults for what lies ahead of them. I wanted to know how prepared they are to enter the real world after graduation, and I immersed myself in a quest to find the answer.

I discovered that high school and college graduates are more equipped to live and succeed on their own than their predecessors were as little as a decade ago. Graduates today know they must excel, and most expect to do well. However, I also found that many young adults have unrealistic expectations and are unprepared.

The number of young adults pursing higher education is on the rise, and many students participate in meaningful internships or related work experience prior to graduation. While this is encouraging, a clear understanding of the dynamics of corporate life seems to be missing from most students' knowledge, according to Rock Anderson, Director of Recruiting Services and Diversity for Siemens Corporation. This includes understanding the politics of corporate life and the importance of seeking and gaining mentorship.

Parents are focused on managing their own busy lives, school counselors and teachers are working at maximum capacity, and employers haven't the time to train the recent graduate in need of continuing education. Through her work with employers and teens, Renee Ward, founder of Teens4hire.org, has found that the majority of young adults have very little knowledge about the basic rules of the workplace. When high school students were asked how many times it is acceptable to be late for work before it becomes a problem for an employer, the majority said eight or nine times. When asked if it is appropriate to leave the workplace without asking to handle a personal emergency, most said yes.

In the real world, arriving late for work is *never* acceptable, nor is leaving unannounced, despite the reason.

After graduation, students are expected to become responsible young adults who move smoothly into their work and home communities, but many still feel and act like children. They may have advanced degrees, a fancy resume, and answers to tough interview questions, but they lack the confidence to look an interviewer in the eye or the common sense to turn off their cell phone during a meeting.

Life as an adult is much different from life as a student. In school, if you do enough to get by, you'll pass. The more you study and the harder you work, the better the grade you'll receive. Although standards for graduation have changed over the years, the objective has remained the same: to meet or exceed the minimum requirements to receive a passing grade.

From kindergarten to graduation, academic and personal success is measured by a report card. In elementary school, equal emphasis is placed on the skills we learn and the way we behave. As we progress, we are expected to understand the code of conduct and behave appropriately. Once the conduct portion of the report card is removed, we are graded solely on our knowledge. Students gain merit solely through their academic achievements.

After years of grading, ranking, and assessing, report cards disappear. Recent graduates, who for the most part have identified themselves through their academic success, are thrust into the mainstream, receiving little or no feedback along the way. At some point, the question, "How am I doing?" requires an answer.

Paychecks and pay raises replace report cards and become the only tangible measure of success. However, neither guarantees the personal satisfaction of a job well done or a balanced and meaningful life.

Graduates rightly assume that more lies ahead for them than working and collecting a paycheck, but when dreams begin to fade and goals seem unattainable, no degree can provide the solution. Grade point average and class rank do not guarantee a life of health, wealth, or successful relationships.

The more complex life becomes, the more difficult it is to evaluate our progress. When faced with mounting responsibilities, it's easy to lose sight of what's important. If we thrive in our careers, we consider ourselves successful. Money and power can be addicting. The praise and respect we receive through our achievements sustain us and provide the personal acknowledgement we crave.

Once we've made the grade, we persevere; we focus on our work while neglecting ourselves and our relationships. It may take years to realize the impact of our neglect, and by the time we do, it may be too late to change the damage that's been done.

School report cards may vanish, but the grading continues; *we are evaluated throughout our entire lives.* The grading system becomes more complex, and we often lack the information we need to do well.

In the real world, we are graded on our *skills*: work skills, communication skills, leadership skills, and social skills. We also are graded on our *behavior*: We're expected to practice self-discipline, work well with others, and have a positive attitude.

There are many unspoken expectations in life, and they come in the form of an unwritten code of conduct. The astute catch on by observing, while others quickly fall behind. Meeting the minimum requirements of this code may be enough for some, but for those who seek an *extraordinary* life, doing enough to get by simply isn't enough.

Earning a degree is an accomplishment, and one to be proud of, but it does not prepare anyone for all that lies ahead, nor does it increase the odds of living a successful, meaningful, or happy life.

Every family, every home, every school, and every community has a code of conduct. As graduates move away from their roots and become members of the real world, they are presented with a new code: the code of conduct *for life.*

Everyone is expected to abide by this code, and anyone can follow it. Those who do will have an advantage, and those who do not will suffer the consequences. Until now, this code has only been *implied*. Now that it's expressed, you can keep it and refer to it anytime you need to.

There are seven sections in this book. Each section represents a different set of skills to master. While some people might emphasize the significance of one section over another, each section and every tip is of equal importance.

The 101 tips in this book came from an initial list of over 200 tips. To make sure I selected the most important tips, I solicited input from people of all walks of life, and they enthusiastically responded.

My request for advice for new graduates struck a chord with people who have genuine concerns about young adults and their ability to make it on their own. Many were happy to share their own tips, words of wisdom, and lessons learned.

I received responses from business executives, entrepreneurs, and employees from a variety of industries. Ideas were sent in from stay-at-home parents, teachers, writers, lawyers, doctors, musicians, and young adults themselves. Responses came from near and far and from all parts of the world. I am deeply touched by the number of people who took time to reply to my request. Their responses were thoughtful, insightful, and candid. You will find portions of some of the comments I received in a special quotes section in the back of this book.

You can use this book in a variety of ways. Read it from cover to cover, or start reading the section, or tip, that interests you most. It's your book and your life. After reading each tip in its entirety, you can reinforce the concept by glancing through the tip titles.

This book is written for graduates starting out in life, but it serves as a valuable tool for *anyone*. Some books are meant to be read and enjoyed; others are intended to be read and applied. This book is a little of both. I hope you enjoy what you read and that you live your life differently as a result. My life changed from writing this book, and I know yours can change from reading it.

—Susan Morem

If you have a tip, a personal story to share, or advice you'd like to pass along to be included in a future edition of this book, please send your tips to: tips@tipsforgrads.com.

Work Skills

Find a Job and Achieve Career Success

TIP # I
**It's no longer about the grades you make;
it's whether or not you make the grade.**

Congratulations graduate! The time has come for you to say goodbye to your life as a student and hello to your life as an adult. As an adult, you don't have teachers to answer to, tests to study for, or grades to make. Your year isn't divided into quarters or semesters, and, unless you go back to school, you don't have to look at a report card *ever* again.

Welcome to the real world! In the real world, you'll find that success isn't measured with an A or a B; success is about learning, then living, your new ABCs.

Real world ABCs: Your code of conduct for life.

A **is for Adult:** You're an adult now for the rest of your life. As an adult, people expect you to *look, act,* and *dress* professionally and appropriately. It *does* matter what people think of you now. Maintaining your individuality is great—and encouraged. But a certain amount of conformity and maturity in appearance and behavior is expected.

B **is for Better:** Be better than you need to be. You are a work in progress—become a student of life. Be someone for whom good isn't good enough. Look for new ways of doing things, and don't be afraid of change. Strive to improve yourself professionally and personally every single day.

C is for Control: Take control of your life; don't let life control you. Decide what you want. Don't be wishy-washy. Life is not a dress rehearsal; every decision you make will either move you toward your goals or push you away from them. Make good decisions. As comedian Tim Allen once said, "If you don't make decisions in life, life will make decisions for you."

D is for Dream: Dare to *dream*. Dare to dream the *impossible* dream. If you dream it, you can create it; it depends on what you're *willing* to do. Don't listen to people who try to destroy your dreams. Most likely, someone tried to spoil theirs and probably succeeded. If you don't think dreams are possible, ask anyone whose impossible dreams came true. They'll tell you dreams really do come true.

E is for Enthusiasm: Enthusiasm matters a great deal. Enthusiasm is contagious. Infect the people you work with; create a more pleasurable, meaningful work environment. If you aren't enthusiastic about what you're doing, consider doing something else. Life is too short to curb your enthusiasm.

F is for Failure: When you fail in school, you are *held* back; when you fail in life, you are *set* back. Failure is temporary and is nothing to be embarrassed about. Some of the greatest victories are a result of the worst defeats. Everyone faces personal struggles, failures, and moments of truth. Be a student of your own failure. There's no shame in failing; the shame is in not trying.

G is for Give: Be known as a giver, not a taker. Make a difference in someone's life; pay a compliment, do something nice, and volunteer. When you give to simply give, with no strings attached, you always end up getting more back. Try it and see for yourself.

H is for Happy: If you can wake up every day and be happy with yourself, your relationships, and your job, you are living life at its best. I know it isn't easy; there's always something to gripe about or problems that get in the way. Abraham Lincoln once said most people are about as happy as they make their minds up to be. Don't complain; forget about your problems. Make your mind up to be happy.

I is for Invest: Invest in your future *now*. Just because you're making money doesn't mean you have to spend it all. Learn from the millions of people who wish they had *invested* their money rather than thrown it away. Don't spend *more* than you earn; spend less. Stay out of debt and *invest in yourself.*

J is for Joyfulness: Find joy and meaning in everything you do. Find joy making others joyful; make your day by making someone else's day. Call the store clerk, the driver, or the receptionist by name, and ask about his or her day. Then watch the response you receive. Reach out to others and make a personal connection; then feel and see joyfulness at its best.

K is for Knowledge: You may be done with your formal education, but some of your best lessons are yet to be learned. Become a *lifelong* learner; be a student of *life*. I heard this saying years ago: *The more you know, the more you know you don't know.* The older I get, the more I understand it. Know that you don't yet know all you need to know. Seek knowledge and learn something new every chance you get.

L is for Listen: There is a reason we all have two ears and only one mouth. Use yours proportionately. Listening is more than hearing. You are responsible for getting what someone's telling you, so listen carefully.

M is for Mistake: Make mistakes; make *lots* of *new* mistakes. It's the best way for you to learn. Don't be afraid—*everyone makes mistakes.* Let your mistakes get you down. Take some time to grieve over, not *gloss* over, what you learned from your mistake. Then get back up, and strive to never repeat the same mistake.

N is for No: Know how to say no. Say no to overindulgence, say no to risky behavior, say no to your bad habits, and say no to the toxic people you meet. Know when and how to say no and *mean* it.

O is for Opportunity: Opportunity sometimes knocks very quietly. If you listen, you will hear when opportunity knocks at your door. Pay attention to everything you see and hear. Take risks, seize opportunities, and create your own good fortune.

P is for Patience: Like Rome, your career won't be built in a day. Everyone starts somewhere, and everything takes time. Although it may be difficult to understand now, you really will enjoy and appreciate what you have much more if you have to work for it and toward it. Patience really *is* a virtue. Be patient. The best is yet to come.

Q is for Quality: Put a stamp of quality on *everything* you do. Seek quality relationships, buy quality clothes, eat quality food, get a quality job, be a quality person, turn in quality work, and think quality thoughts. Remember, it's not quantity you want; it's quality. Live a quality life.

R is for Reputation: Your permanent record, for the rest of your life, begins *now*. Think about what kind of person you want to be known as in your personal and professional life. A gossip? A backbiter? Someone who will step on others to get where he or she wants to be? Think of your reputation as your little shadow, because it will follow you *wherever* you go. Take care to cultivate a reputation that you can live with for the rest of your life.

S is for **Success:** Success isn't measured by the title you have, the money you make, or the value of your possessions. Success is what you make of your *life*. If you compare yourself to others, you will always fall short. Compare yourself to *your* goals and desires; you have everything you need to succeed.

T is for **Thankful:** Be thankful; appreciate the opportunity to work, and do your best, regardless of the position. No job is beneath you. Any job that's legal is honorable and probably pays you more in a month than people in many parts of the world make in a year. Be thankful for your health, your family, and all the goodness you see every day.

U is for **Understanding people:** Understand that people matter; *all* people. Always remember the people who helped you. Always try to help others. Treat *everyone* with respect, regardless of status or position. As you mature, you will come to realize that it's not who you *know* but who you *are*.

V is for **Values:** Identify your values; know what's important to you in life, and never compromise the things you value most. Take a stand for what you believe. If you *stand* for nothing, you'll *fall* for everything.

W is for **Willing:** Be willing to stay late, come in early, skip going out for lunch, or whatever it takes to get the job done well and on time. Most important, be willing to start at the bottom and work your way up; everyone has to start somewhere.

X is for "X"traordinary: Some things happen for no reason at all, with no warning and no explanation. You can think you've got the world in the palm of your hand, but when something unexpected happens, you learn you do not. Never become so smug that you think you're infallible. You are not. Live your life and go for your dreams, but never take your health, your family, your country, your job, or *anything* for granted.

Y is for You: You are enough. Don't focus on those who have more than you; help out those who have less. Don't feel bad for what you *don't* get to do; be glad for what you get. Don't live your life regretfully; envision a bright future ahead.

Z is for Zoom: Get ready, get set... zoom! Enjoy the ride of your life. There's a wide-open road ahead of you now; follow the road to your dreams.

TIP # 2
Your first job is finding a job.

If you aren't working, technically you are unemployed, but theoretically, you do have a job; your job is to find a job. Whether you realize it or not, you are now self-employed; you've got a job to do, but there's no time clock you need to punch or supervisor you must report to. You're free to begin and end your day as early or as late as you choose and are responsible for setting your goals and tracking your progress. You can put as much or as little effort into your job search as you want, because the only person you have to answer to is yourself. Your success (or lack of it) is up to you, and if things don't go well, there's no one to blame but yourself.

Think of your job search as one of your first entrepreneurial experiences. You are about to begin an adventure in which you'll experience good days and bad days, highs and lows, and ups and downs. Your moods are likely to fluctuate, and your feelings of exuberance, empowerment, and excitement will probably be intertwined with feelings of rejection, loneliness, and, at times, desperation. You will fail before you succeed, and there will be times you'll feel like giving up. But you won't give up. You know you need a job to live the life you choose, so you'll reassure yourself that what you are experiencing is normal; considering that the length of the average job search spans months, not weeks, you will remind yourself that finding a job takes time. It won't take long before your enthusiasm to find a job returns and you are inspired once again to pursue your dreams.

Anything worth having in life is worth pursuing, and to have a job you'll look forward to each day, you'll need to work hard to find it. The secret to a successful job search is to take it seriously and treat it like a job by devoting a significant amount of time to it each day.

You'll need to create a work area devoted to your job search "business." Your ideal office should include a desk, chair, telephone, answering machine, fax machine, printer, planning calendar, computer, and Internet connection. If you don't have all of the equipment you need, find a resource to use; don't be shy about asking family and friends or using the school resource center. You will be most effective when you are organized and prepared. Make sure you have plenty of working pens and pencils, pads of paper, file folders, copies of your resume, and letters of reference on hand at all times.

Because you are your own boss, you can work whatever hours you want, but since you need to connect with potential employers, you'd be wise to work during regular business hours. Go to bed at a reasonable hour and set your alarm clock to wake you in the morning. When your workday begins, turn off the television, stereo, and instant messaging, and minimize your time spent on the phone or in person with friends during business hours.

During your temporary job search career, work on developing new skills and good work habits. Whether you have meetings scheduled for the day or not, get out of your pajamas in the morning and get dressed for work. It will be much easier for you to take yourself and your business seriously and will improve your chances of sounding professional over the phone if you look and feel as though you are a professional businessperson.

There are many ways to go about finding a job; use a variety of resources. Don't hesitate to call a company you want to work for to request an informational interview. Every day, you should generate new leads for yourself and make new contacts. Tell everyone you know you are looking for work, but never rely on anyone else to get you a job; it's *your* job to find work and no one can do it for you.

When you find yourself waiting for the phone to ring, pick it up and make a call, then another and another. While you never want to become a pest to anyone, you must pursue the job you want and set yourself apart from others who are vying for the same position.

When you treat looking for a job like a job, before you know it, you will have a real job to go to every day. And if you work hard at getting the job you *want*, chances are you'll land a job you really *like*. It's worth the extra effort.

TIP # 3

Get a makeover. Student fashion is "out" in the office.

You probably already know that image is important.

You know how good you feel when you're wearing the perfect pair of jeans, shoes that fit just right, and an oversized, cozy sweatshirt embroidered with your school logo. Surely you have a few nice outfits reserved for special occasions, but most likely your preferred uniform during your time as a student has been jeans or sweats. You've probably never worn one of your special occasion outfits (something you'd wear to prom or out on New Year's Eve) to class or on a day you were running errands, and you'd never wear jeans or sweats to an interview or a job—or would you?

Think of the stares people get when their image strays too far from the norm. Perhaps you take a second look when you spot someone with purple hair, black lips, or covered with metal chains. You know a person's image is important, but do you know just how important it is when applying for a job or establishing yourself as a credible business person? Have you thought about the image you need to project as you transform yourself from a professional student to an employable professional?

If you think that dressing nicely is what matters and are planning on wearing your special occasion outfits to work, think again. If your skirt is short, your neckline plunging, shoes too clunky, heels too high, pants too tight or so big they're falling off, your special outfits should be saved for special occasions that have nothing to do with your work or career.

When you're looking for employment, student fashion is "out" and career fashion is "in." It's time for you to do an image makeover.

You may face many obstacles, money being one of them. You might not feel you can afford to buy new clothes, but you can't afford not to. You don't need to purchase an entirely new wardrobe, but you do need to have at least one good suit to wear to interviews and a few additional pieces to mix and match. You don't want to wear the same outfit every day or show up at the second and third interview looking as though you never change your clothes.

You can build your work-wardrobe over time by purchasing just a few items at a time. No one will notice when you are wearing the same pair of dark slacks you wore the day before as long as you change the shirt, jacket, or accessories you wear with them. A few basic pieces are all you need to get started.

As you create your new image, consider the nature of the industry you will be working in when deciding how formally or informally you will dress. Even casual workplaces have guidelines; what's considered appropriate casual wear for work is much different from the casual attire you've been accustomed to. Become familiar with the dress code in the company and industry you work in. Always dress a little better than you need to; it will help you establish yourself as a person the company should hire.

Purchase the best-quality clothing you can afford. You're better off owning fewer articles of *quality* clothing than a large quantity of poor quality. When you shop for work clothes, avoid trendy styles. It's important to look up to date, but you don't need to wear all the latest fashions. Classic clothing will be a better investment, and you will be able to wear your clothes longer if you buy items that don't go out of style quickly. You can look professional without sacrificing your sense of style. Build your wardrobe slowly, and look at the way successful people in your field dress for guidance.

Watch for sales and special discounts, and you should never have to pay full price for your business clothes. If you need help with your shopping, ask a salesclerk, mentor, or trusted friend. Always consult a tailor (you can find one in a phone directory) to ensure your clothing fits properly. Stay away from clothing that is too tight, too loose, too short, too long, too youthful, or provocative. Looking sexy will not help you look professional; save it for nonwork-related activities. You don't want your body to be the focus of attention, and it will be if you emphasize it.

Your hair, makeup, hands, nails, shoes, briefcase, and accessories also play an important role in your new image. Long hair and nails, high heels, clunky shoes, gaudy jewelry, and trendy styles all diminish your efforts to appear more professional. People are likely to respond negatively to visible tattoos and face or body piercings, so do what you can to cover up.

The way you look sends a message to others. If you don't care enough to pay attention to your appearance, people will think you don't care about anything and won't pay attention to you. If you don't look as though you take yourself or your career seriously, no one will take you seriously either. If you look like you are still in school, you won't look as though you are ready for the business world, and you will reduce your chances of a job offer or promotion.

When your image reflects your confidence, ability, ambition, and desire to succeed, it will be obvious to others. You won't have to work as hard to convince others of your intentions because they will be apparent.

If you look like a student, you'll be treated like a student. If you look like you're stuck in the past, you'll miss out on future opportunities. But if you look successful, you'll increase your chances of becoming successful. Never, ever, underestimate the power of your image.

TIP # 4
Practice makes perfect; rehearse before you interview.

Few things are as nerve-wracking as a job interview. You know your words will be scrutinized and your demeanor evaluated. You want to be yourself, but it's not easy when you feel as though you're trying to be someone else. You're going to be on stage in one of the most important performances of your life, so it's natural to feel a little jittery, but rehearsing will help ease your nerves.

Think of yourself as the lead actor in a play. You are playing a job seeker. Since you have the starring role, you'll need to do what any actor would do to prepare: Do plenty of research to understand the premise of the story, change your appearance to convincingly portray the character you are playing, and rehearse, rehearse, rehearse.

You'll need an understanding of the setting of each scene and the characteristics of the character you will play. To prepare for a role, some actors will gain or lose weight, cut or color their hair, grow a beard, or shave a mustache, all in an attempt to look and feel authentic.

The storyline: You are looking for a dream job. The job market is competitive and you're a little apprehensive. You know how important each interview is and want to determine what you need to do to feel better about your interviews and get the results you desire.

Research: You need to research the industry and company prior to every interview. You'll enhance your performance when you are knowledgeable about the company you are interviewing with. An understanding of the company's background, mission and purpose, products and services, corporate culture, headquarters and locations, and its competition is essential. When possible, speak directly with employees of the company to gain an understanding of what it is like to work there. Your preparation will be obvious to the interviewer; you will talk in specifics rather than generalities, and you will respond to and ask questions with ease.

Background of script: Although every interview will differ, some aspects will be quite similar. You'll be asked questions, and your answers will determine how well you do. You need to have several responses prepared and memorized in advance so you are not caught off guard. You should tailor your responses to each question and industry. You need to know what's on your resume because you may be asked to talk about it, and you must be prepared to tell your story briefly when you are asked to talk about yourself. This story is not intended to be a detailed life history but a summary of what you're all about. Practice telling your story, because it must be relayed in a minute or less.

You need to identify your strengths and weaknesses and reasons for both, what makes you unique, and the reason you want to work for the company you are interviewing with. You must be prepared to talk about your outside interests, experiences, goals, and plans for the future.

The setting: Most interviews will take place in an office setting, but a few will be conducted over the phone, in a boardroom, at a restaurant, or in other public places. Whenever possible, become familiar with the setting of your interview ahead of time. A trial run ensures you will be able to find the place when you need to, and you will be able to visualize the interview during your rehearsal. Know how to conduct yourself and eliminate distractions when on the phone, and brush up on your table manners before you hit the restaurant scene.

Wardrobe: You need to look like a polished, professional, and successful business person, so business attire is a must. Whether you are male or female, a conservative business suit will be your best choice. Pay attention to detail; make sure the suit fits and is clean and well pressed and that your shoes are shined.

Hair and makeup: Hair should be freshly cut and styled, clean and combed. Women should wear subtle makeup, and men should be clean-shaven.

Accessories: Few accessories are necessary. Men and women should wear a small to medium watch and no more than one ring on each hand. Men should remove all earrings; women can wear small earrings, but no more than one per ear. Any additional accessories should be kept to a minimum.

Props: A small to medium briefcase in good condition, a professional-looking pen in working condition, a pad of paper, and copies of resumes. If you take your cell phone to the interview, be sure to turn it off. The risk of having it ring in the middle of a scene (or interview) is too high.

Body movement, expression, and posture: Your goal is to play someone confident, assertive, and comfortable with him or herself and others. You can accomplish this by standing and sitting tall, your shoulders back and your head held high and straightforward. Offer your hand for a handshake and shake briefly and firmly. Walk slowly and deliberately, keep your hands out of your pockets, and don't fidget or play with your hair, rings, or pen. Keep your eyes on the person you are speaking with, glancing away only occasionally. Vary your facial expressions; smile, raise your eyebrows, tilt your head, nod in agreement, and do everything you can to appear interested in the person and conversation.

Vocal intonation: Speak at a moderate pace with vocal variety and inflection. Avoid being loud or too quiet. A mid-lower tone will help convey confidence. Practice making statements sound like statements, not questions. In other words, avoid lifting your voice, as you do when you're asking a question, *unless* you're asking a question.

Practice and rehearsal schedule: Hold as many practice sessions as possible, and keep practicing until you are sure you have the look, moves, and script mastered. Practice your lines by yourself and with others. You should have at least one dress rehearsal and get a friend to videotape it. I highly recommend you view and review your video several times, both with and without sound. When you watch it without sound, you'll focus on the message you send nonverbally. Watching your own performance is the best way to critique and, ultimately, improve it.

TIP # 5
Get in the driver's seat.

Ruth used to drive everywhere. She drove cross-country for her vacations and drove over 2000 miles to her son's wedding. Her fear of flying kept her on the ground, driving everywhere she went. When her health problems prohibited her from driving long distances, she sought professional help to overcome her fear of flying. She learned how to cope with her fear and came to realize her fear of *losing control* had been controlling her.

The need to control and the fear of losing control can do funny things to people. Many people say the best way to conquer a fear is by facing it. Yet fear can be overpowering, and sometimes it's easier to give in to our fears than it is to take control of our lives.

Don't let your fear of failure, rejection, embarrassment, or *any* fear paralyze you. Take control of yourself, your life, and your career. Everyone has fears, and you must identify and face yours. Where did the fear originate? Is it *helping* you or holding you back? Are you willing to do whatever it takes to control the fear you have?

You can drive your life or let it drive you; you can be either a driver or a passenger of life. You can go where you want or let others take you where they think you ought to be.

Don't depend on others for your happiness or success. You're on your own now, and it's up to you to take your life in the direction you choose. It's not easy making decisions when you're insecure and afraid of making a mistake. Trust yourself. *No one* knows what's better for you than *you* do.

If you can't find a job, create one. If you want more knowledge, seek it. You can accomplish anything you set your mind to. Only you can determine the course of your life.

Steps to a successful road trip through life:

Get in the driver's seat: Take control of your life and career.

Ignite your imagination: Dare to dream. Imagine anything is possible.

Determine your course: Make a plan. You won't end up where you want to be if you don't create a roadmap to help you get there.

Watch for signs along the way: Pay attention to the people you meet and the obstacles you encounter; there is a reason they will surface. You can learn something from everyone you meet and everything that happens.

Proceed with caution: This is your life; handle it with care. Never become so focused on driving that you bypass opportunities or overlook the most important people in your life.

You are about to embark on the trip of your life. Many people discover that the journey is much more exciting than the destination—enjoy your journey!

TIP # 6

First impressions create lasting impressions.

Can you remember the anticipation you felt each year on the first day of school? The moment you walked into the classroom, you began evaluating your teachers and classmates. Before the day started, you probably had a good idea about whether or not you thought you liked what you saw or whether it was going to be a good year.

As you search for a job or start a new one, the anticipation you feel might remind you of the way you felt the first day of school; you're embarking on a new experience, meeting new people, and evaluating your new situation. With just a glance, you will make assumptions about the people you meet and they will make assumptions about you. Your (and their) instantaneous conclusions and decisions based on first impressions will affect your future. First impressions last much longer than the time it takes to form them.

The moment you enter a room and the instant you meet someone, the evaluation process begins. If you are dressed inappropriately or sloppily, are disorganized, or look worried, negative assumptions will be made before you have a chance to say hello. Business people are busy people, with little time to spare. No one is going to waste time getting to know someone who appears incapable or uncaring. Most interviews, meetings, and interactions are under time constraints. If you fail to make a positive impression within the brief amount of time you are given, you may never get another chance.

You can't afford to have a bad day or an off moment; every interaction you experience is critical. When you know what kind of impression you want to make and are able to convey it effectively to others, you increase your chances of getting the job you want and establishing yourself as a competent professional.

You're competing with others who match your knowledge and ability, but you can differentiate yourself by the way you look, act, and connect with others by doing the following:

- Create a plan; identify your objectives and how to achieve them.

- Consider the industry and corporate culture to help you determine what to wear.

- Dress to impress the people you meet.

- Carry yourself confidently; act confident even if you don't feel confident.

- Hold your head high and look forward.

- Walk slowly and purposefully.

- Greet everyone you meet.

- Shake hands firmly.

- Make direct, consistent eye contact.

- Practice and prepare.

The more prepared you are, the better your chances of making a positive impression. When you are prepared, you will feel better and be more present. You will find people are willing to take the time to get to know you, and you will get to know people on a deeper level.

It takes only seconds to form an impression, but the impact is long lasting. Know what kind of impression you want to make and do everything you can to create it *every* time you interact with another person.

TIP # 7

Timing is everything.

If you are a job seeker and are dissatisfied with your interview results, changing the time of your interviews may be all you need to do. The results of a survey developed by Accountemps, a temporary staffing service, suggest job seekers schedule early morning interviews in order to have an advantage in the hiring process. More than two thirds of the financial officers of accounting firms polled said the most productive time for meeting with applicants is between 9:00 A.M. and 11:00 A.M.

When you want to reach someone by phone, try to determine the best time to call. You may have to learn by trial and error or ask someone to help you out. Don't hesitate to ask a receptionist or the person you'll be calling when you get the chance. You might prefer to make calls midmorning, but if the person you need to reach is in meetings by then, you're out of luck. When you call at different times, you'll increase your chances of making a connection.

Years ago, I tried and tried to reach the busy CEO of a company but was having difficulty getting through to him. One night I had worked late and although it was after business hours and I was sure he had gone home, I decided to call him one more time. I was shocked when he answered his phone, and he was impressed I was calling as late as I was. He rarely answered his phone and was very selective in the calls he took, but since he was the only one working that night, he answered. Change your pattern of calling to increase your chances of reaching someone.

Dee, a television producer, missed an opportunity of a lifetime the morning she was late for work. One of the hosts of the show she produced became ill and a replacement was needed. By the time Dee arrived, a co-host was found, but the minute the executive producer saw her he expressed his regret. "Dee," he said "where were you when I needed you? You would have been the *perfect* guest host!" Dee missed what she says was a once in a lifetime opportunity that never presented itself again. Be on time: You can't seize the chance of a lifetime if you're not there to grab it.

Arriving a few minutes late to work or to a business event is *not* okay. A workday that begins at 8:00 A.M. begins precisely at that time—not five or ten minutes later. A meeting called for 10:00 A.M. should begin at that time. Arriving five minutes early sends a completely different message from showing up five minutes late.

You may think its no big deal to run a few minutes behind, but to your employer it is. Consistently showing up late for work can cost you your job or future opportunities. Unless you have a good reason, showing up late for an interview will usually work against you and may disqualify you.

Always leave room in your schedule to catch up if you need to. Expect the unexpected. There will be bad weather that causes poor driving conditions. There will also be traffic delays and times when you get lost. Allow time for these things. You are better off arriving someplace early, with time to use the restroom, make a phone call, or review your notes, than making your entrance in a tizzy.

If you say you will get back to someone by the end of the day, make sure you get back to that person by the end of the day. People are counting on you and have deadlines to meet. Be realistic about your time. Know what you will be able to accomplish within the time you have. Making promises and commitments you cannot fulfill will lead to disappointment in yourself and others. Be honest with yourself and others. Telling someone in advance you will need more time to do something is better than saying you will have something done that you fail to do.

Time is a precious commodity; spend your time doing the things that matter. Become aware of your timing and work with your natural rhythm. We all have certain times we are most energetic, sluggish, and tired. Plan your activities around the times you function best. If you're most energetic in the morning, use that time to get things done that take energy. Save your easier tasks for those times you feel less energized.

Time favors no one; we all have the same amount of time to use each day. Managing your time effectively requires planning and discipline. Invest in a personal planning system and learn time management skills *now*. Consider taking a time management class or seminar to learn techniques that will benefit you the rest of your life.

Don't let time control you; take control of your time. When you respect time, you show respect for yourself and others. Use your time wisely. The difference between coming close to your dreams and reaching them is often a matter of timing.

TIP # 8
Go to work every day as if it were the first day of your job.

It's the day you begin your first real job. Finally, the moment you've been preparing for has arrived. The excitement you feel, combined with your desire to learn and do well, will make your first day one of your best. You'll wake up extra early and give yourself plenty of time to get ready. You'll select one of your nicer outfits to wear in your effort to make a really good impression and will leave a few minutes early to assure you arrive on time.

You'll smile at the people you see, offer to help others, and ask lots of questions to make sure you do everything right. You'll be excited to share the details of your day with your family and friends and decide you like the way it feels to be a part of the real world. You'll be excited the day you receive your first paycheck, which will be a substantial increase from what you've made in the past.

I hope the exhilaration you feel at the start of your career will last, but, sadly, over time, some people lose the excitement they once held for their work. The joy they felt toward their job diminishes, and their desire to learn and do well is replaced by their desire to simply get through the day.

Imagine this: You no longer feel the need to make a good impression, so you stay in bed until the last possible moment you can. You rush to get ready for work, and you bypass the nicer outfit for the dreary one that reflects your dull mood. You don't really care that you've arrived a few minutes late, and you don't bother acknowledging the people you see. You watch the clock as the time slowly passes each day, and by the time you arrive home you're too tired to talk about your day and don't have much to say anyway.

I sincerely hope you will never experience job burnout, but unfortunately, many people do. Some people become overwhelmed by their responsibilities; others lose their gusto and no longer try. Sometimes physical problems lead to burn-out, but more often than not, it's the *attitude problems* that do.

As you get more comfortable in your environment, the excitement of the first day will decrease, and the pressures of life will increase. Not everyone will burn out; you can and should enjoy the work you do throughout your entire career. Never forget how hard you worked to get the job you have or the excitement you felt on your very first day. When you go to work everyday as if it were your first day on the job, your days will be brighter. As a result, you will shine brightly too.

TIP # 9
Proofread *every* document.

You've spent hours preparing and perfecting your resume. Each time you send it out, you hope it will do its job and you will be called for an interview. When the phone doesn't ring, you wonder why; you know you have ideal qualifications for several of the positions you applied for. When you spoke directly with one of the hiring managers, he told you he'd be moving quickly to set up interviews. You *know* he was interested in you, especially when he asked to see your resume right away. So what are these companies looking for if they're not looking for the most qualified person?

Companies *do* want the most qualified person, but if that person's resume or cover letter has an error, the sloppiness ruins his chances for an interview. A resume or letter that's crumpled, spotted, or stained will *not* represent you well, nor will one with typos or grammatical errors. You might overlook these things, but a potential employer will *not*.

Seventy-six percent of human resource professionals said they would remove an applicant from consideration for a job if they found a typo or grammatical error on a cover letter or resume, a survey conducted by The Society for Human Resource Management revealed.

You've reviewed your resume 100 times. You've read and reread the cover letter you sent. You can't understand why you didn't catch the mistake, but don't be too hard on yourself; it happens all the time.

We're often too close to our own documents and unable to view them objectively. We rush to meet deadlines or finish a project, leaving little time to catch our mistakes. And at times, we are simply careless; we don't bother checking the documents we send.

It pays to proofread your resume and *every* document you create. Typos, grammatical errors, and misspelled words aren't the only problems you'll find. When you write something, you know what you're trying to say, but others do not.

Robert Half, founder of Accountemps, uses the term "resumania" to describe the blunders found in resumes, job applications, and cover letters. The following examples are from Half's resumania file *(and my reaction to each)*:

- I am entirely through in my work; no detail gets by me. *(I can see that.)*

- Computer Illiterate. *(Too bad, because your other qualifications look good.)*

- Thank you for beeting me for an interview. *(I didn't, but you're welcome.)*

- Planned and held up meetings. *(Did you serve time?)*

- Worked party-time as an office assistant. *(Sounds fun.)*

What would your reaction be if you read any of the preceding errors on a resume or cover letter?

One mistake is all it takes to prevent you from getting an interview, and if you make too many mistakes once you *have* a job, you might find yourself looking for another one sooner than you think. Proofread *all* your e-mails, memos, and letters before sending them.

Check and double-check your work for accuracy, spelling, and errors. The time you spend up front will save you time and *embarrassment* later on. When you are careless in your work, you create problems for yourself and others. You'll end up working harder, redoing things, and dealing with problems *you* created.

Mistakes are costly; proofreading pays.

- Proofread all documents several times.
- Print the document and then read it.
- Read it out loud.
- Walk away from it for awhile; take a break and then come back to it.
- Sleep on it; come back to it the next day.
- Have someone else read it *to* you.
- Have someone else read it *for* you.

TIP # 10

There's nothing more disruptive than being interrupted.

You arrive at work a little early to catch up on some of your work that's been piling up. As your coworkers begin to arrive and stop to say hello, you feel your momentum begin to slow. Your phone rings, your computer dings, and a coworker asks you for help. It's still early in the day, yet you feel yourself growing tense.

There's nothing more disruptive than being interrupted. Constant interruptions, no matter how brief, can interfere with your thought process and ability to complete a project on time. Some interruptions are inevitable and you'll never be able to avoid them entirely, but you can take steps to reduce the number of needless interruptions you have.

Just as others interrupting you is disruptive, so is you interrupting others. Think twice before you interrupt someone else;

become more aware of your tendency to disrupt someone, and know the difference between an interruption that is self-serving or due to a critical matter.

An interruption is *preventable* when:

You ask a question or ask for information you could answer or obtain yourself, respectively.

You want something irrelevant to the person you are interrupting.

The issue can wait until later.

It's unimportant.

An interruption is *unpreventable* when:

Your boss, supervisor, or other authority says it is.

It's life threatening.

There's a medical emergency.

There's a family emergency.

● You're dealing with a work-related crisis.

You risk losing a customer and need to resolve a customer-related predicament.

The matter is time sensitive and vitally important to the person or company.

Prevent other disruptions:

Hang a "Do not disturb" or other sign on your door, wall, or desk.

Alert others: Tell people you will be unavailable in your outgoing voicemail greeting, in person, or by using the out of office reply on your e-mail.

- Leave your office; find another place to do your work.
- Tell the interrupter you can't talk now, and then offer to set a time to meet later.
- When someone approaches, stand up.
- When someone interrupts you, ask, "What can I do for you?"
- When someone asks you to do something, ask, "When do you need to have this done?"
- Remove all extra chairs near your desk.
- When someone interrupts you, be honest. Say something like, "I'm really busy now. Is this something that can wait until later?" or "I'm on a deadline. Can you come back at three o'clock?"
- Turn off the ringer on your phone.
- Leave an informative outgoing voice mail message and e-mail response; if you are working on a deadline and won't be returning calls that day, let others know.
- Turn off the sound on your computer.
- Reserve time to get your work done.
- Establish set hours for interruptions; let others know when interruptions are interfering with your ability to do your work.

Avoid disrupting others:

- A phone call is an interruption to someone; don't make a call unless you have a valid reason.
- When you call, be brief. Ask if you are calling at a good time. If so, state the reason for your call, stick to your purpose, and hang up.

● Be resourceful: If you're looking for information or seeking an answer to a question, try to find what you're looking for yourself.

● Take a break if you need one, but don't bother someone else because you are bored or need a break.

● If you want to talk about your weekend, happy hour, or last night's football game, do it when you share a break with someone or after work.

● If you are upset or feel the need to complain, call a friend. Better yet, let it go and get back to work—you're interrupting yourself.

● If the issue can wait until later, don't interrupt someone now.

● If it's all about you, you're the only one involved, so it's not worth bothering someone else.

TIP # 11

Be willing to make the coffee.

You are in the midst of a job interview and you're feeling good about the way it's progressing. You're proud of the way you've answered the questions you've been asked and confident you will be asked for another interview or offered a job. You sense the interview is coming to a close when the interviewer says he has another question. "Are you willing to make the coffee?" he asks. You're not sure how you should answer.

If you say yes, you wonder if he'll think you're *desperate* for a job, but if you say no, will he think you're uncooperative? How do you think *you* would respond?

If you are faced with a similar question and wonder why it is being asked, it's to determine your willingness to do whatever it takes to help the team, according to Martin Yate, author of the *Knock 'em Dead 2002* job hunting book. Your ability to take direction and work with others is important for an interviewer to know. So is your willingness to start at the bottom, pitch in and help out, do more than what's expected, and remain humble.

When you accept a job, you accept the responsibility that goes with it. Even the most detailed job description can't predict the additional tasks you may occasionally be asked to do.

Your job description may not list housekeeping chores, although you will be expected to do them from time to time. You should always leave things as you found them and pitch in when you see something that needs to be done. If you use the copy or fax machine and use the last of the paper in the tray, you have a choice: You can ignore the empty tray, walk away, and let the next person who uses it refill it, or you can fill it yourself. You may not want to bother, but since you were the one who emptied the paper, you should be willing to refill it. After all, it made it easier on you to have paper in the tray; why not make it easier for someone else?

If you're the first to arrive at work or take the last of the coffee one morning, you can assume more coffee will be consumed. Just because you might have the cup of coffee you want doesn't mean other people shouldn't have theirs. You probably enjoy pouring a cup from a fresh pot and so do others.

The brief amount of time it takes to leave things as (or better than) you found them reaps long-lasting benefits. If you fail to pitch in, you'll become an irritation to others who may become resentful of your refusal to contribute or do your share of the work.

Don't think of these menial tasks as demeaning. No job is beneath you; no matter how deserving you think you are, you are the new kid on the block and are building your reputation. You are being unrealistic if you think you are an exception. Everyone pays his or her dues.

You must be willing to start at the bottom and work your way up. Be willing to make the coffee or to do anything that needs to be done. Don't wait to be asked; just do it. The benefits will be abundant. You will quickly become known as a valuable team member and the kind of person others can depend on. When you are *willing* to do things, you *will* earn the respect you desire because you *did* earn it.

Still wondering how to answer the question? If you are asked if you are willing to make the coffee, say yes! When you are willing to do whatever it takes to get a job done, you'll have a good chance of getting a job.

TIP # 12
You are a product; market yourself.

You're spending the weekend at your friend's cabin. You stop at the store in the small town nearby to pick up a frozen pizza, snacks, and a box of cereal. You're unfamiliar with some of the brands you see, and there are so many choices you're having a difficult time deciding which products to buy.

You finally select a pizza and some munchies but get stuck in the cereal aisle. You see several brands of corn flakes and aren't sure which brand to choose. The brand you usually buy is the most expensive; the least expensive is in a cellophane bag and is a generic brand you've never heard of.

Which cereal will you buy? If advertising and marketing departments are doing their job, you'll either buy the brand you're most familiar with or the one in the package you find most visually appealing.

Packaging is important; there's a reason you wrap the gifts you give with expensive wrap and fancy bows. You could just use a paper bag or cardboard box, but you probably don't. Why? Because when you give a wrapped gift, it is evident you took the time to prepare. In addition, a nicely wrapped gift is much more enticing than one that is not. There is a mystique and feeling of anticipation about what's hidden behind the fancy trappings.

You are a gift; you're smart, motivated, capable, and ambitious. But not everyone knows this about you, and you can't go around telling people how great you are. If you want to know how to get others to notice your gifts, the answer could be in your packaging.

When Jay Lipe, author of *The Marketing Toolkit for Growing Businesses,* began to think of himself as a product while looking for a job, he distinguished himself from other interviewees. His marketing strategy was a result of his unique packaging (how he dressed and acted), positioning, pricing (his salary), and even the copy (words) he used to describe himself. As a result, every time he received a call-back from a company, he knew the company was interested in the unique skills he had successfully marketed.

When he called a woman in the real estate business to request an informational interview, he had no ulterior motive; he simply wanted to learn more about the real estate industry. One week after meeting the woman, she called and offered him a job. He hadn't sought a job, but because she knew he was available she chose the product (him) she felt most comfortable with. Jay's effective marketing and research campaign worked; he had better results from his informational interviews than he did from job interviews!

There's a reason you receive trial-sized samples and a reason ads and commercials are shown repeatedly: *Consumers buy products they are familiar with.*

There's a reason companies invest time and money developing the packaging of a product: *Consumers buy products that are visually appealing.*

There's a reason companies conduct research: *Consumers respond to products that have been marketed effectively to fill a need.*

Steps to creating a marketing plan:

Step 1: Know your target market. Use resource centers, the library, and the Internet to learn more about job and industry trends or to find detailed information about a company. Read industry publications, trade journals, company brochures, and annual reports of the companies you are interested in. *Become as knowledgeable as you can about your market.*

Step 2: Research your consumer. Interview the people you will be *marketing* to. Ask for informational interviews. *Become as knowledgeable as you can about your consumer.*

Step 3: Distinguish yourself. Set yourself apart from your competition. Know what your unique skills and talents are. If you don't know what they are, talk with others who know you and trust you and ask for input. Evaluate your experiences and identify the successes you've had and the lessons you've learned. No matter how insignificant you think something is, it may be the one thing that distinguishes you from others. *Become as knowledgeable as you can about your uniqueness.*

Step 4: Create an attractive package. Your packaging should be based on what your consumer will buy. Keep this in mind when deciding what to wear and determining the manner in which you will behave. *Become as knowledgeable as you can about your consumers' expectations.*

Step 5: Launch a marketing campaign. Use your creativity to come up with multiple methods of marketing. Determine the important selling points and right words; then make phone calls, send mail or e-mail, use the Internet, attend networking events, join a job or other support group, request meetings and informational interviews, and use any other method you can think of. *Become as knowledgeable as you can about the most effective ways to market yourself.*

Step 6: Become a familiar brand name. Keep your name in front of people. Do what you can to stay connected to your consumers. Remember special occasions, call to say hello, or check in occasionally to offer an update on your status. Send thank you notes, a brief e-mail, or a related article you've read. Never become a nuisance, but always look for a reason to keep in touch with your contacts. *Become as knowledgeable as you can about ways to become a familiar brand name.*

TIP # 13
Neatness counts; get organized and stay organized.

Your boss has an important lunch meeting she must attend, and after discovering her car won't start, she asks you if you will drive her to the meeting. As the two of you walk to your car, you begin apologizing for the condition it's in. You regret not stopping at the car wash and wish you had taken the time to drop off the dirty clothes strewn across the back seat of your car. The dangling mirror and missing hubcap never bothered you before, and now you're wondering if your boss will notice. She waits as you remove the clutter from the front seat to make room for her to sit down. You're embarrassed when she sees your briefcase overflowing with papers and the number of empty soda cans and food wrappers in your car. You realize your car looks like a traveling storage shed, and although you hope it doesn't matter, you have a feeling it really does.

Neatness goes beyond personal appearance. The tidier and more organized you are, the more professional and in control you appear. A mess suggests *you* are out of control. The more organized you are, the more efficient you become. Your car, your briefcase, your desk, and everything you surround yourself with affect your ability to find things quickly and influence the perception others have of you.

The ability to find files and papers when you need them will save you time and reduce the stress that can evolve from not being able to find something when you need it. Your work area is not your private domain. It will be seen by others and should be kept neat at all times. You may be able to shut the door to your room at home and overlook the clutter, but your work space is part of a larger environment, and it is important to keep it clean. Papers piled on the floor are not only distracting but could pose a safety issue if you work in a high-traffic area.

Many people will get organized once or twice a year, keep things neat a short while, and return to their original mess. It is important to get organized and equally important to *stay* organized. It doesn't take much time to put things away if you do it consistently.

You will be handling lots of information. Try to handle things only one time before deciding what you will do them. Putting things in a pile you plan to deal with later does nothing but create piles for you to deal with. When a letter, brochure, or memo comes to you, try to handle it only once. Make a decision about what you want to do with it. Do you need to give it to someone else, save it, file it, or throw it away? If you are not sure, put it in a special file or basket that you will go through at the end of the week, after you've had a chance to make a decision. When you go through the pile again, make a decision about each item, and get rid of what you can. Get into the habit of labeling and filing, not piling. Label your folders *and* your papers. Doing so will make it easier for you to find them later. Use baskets to help you sort your papers; you may still have a few piles, but they will be smaller and probably more organized.

Do routine maintenance to save time and minimize frustration. Keep pencils sharpened, staples in your stapler, and all of your tools working. Get rid of old food, containers, cups, and soda cans. Wipe down phones, keyboards, and shelves.

You never know who will notice what. Someone I worked with told me about a time she needed information from a coworker. He told her she'd find it in his computer, but his keyboard was so filthy she didn't want to touch it. Although her coworker was a nice guy, she said that incident changed her entire view of him. She couldn't imagine how anyone could touch that thing!

Neatness counts and is more than simply being neat. Living among clutter can clutter your mind. Take the time you need to get organized, and then stay organized. You'll be glad you did when you get the next promotion or award.

TIP # 14

Do it now, not later; don't become a procrastinator.

When you were in school and given an assignment, did you typically begin working on it right away or wait until you were closer to the deadline to begin? If you had a tendency to wait and often found yourself cramming at the last minute to get an assignment done on time, you are not alone. Many people procrastinate, although some people struggle with procrastination more than others.

When given a choice, most people prefer to do the things they enjoy rather than those they do not. When you are faced with the daunting task of doing something unpleasant, it is easier to put it off than it is to do it. When the consequences of not doing something are worse than the consequences of doing it, however, you're more likely to get it done. Necessity can be a big motivator.

If you know you should look for a job, begin a project, or confront someone about a problem, but doing so is difficult or makes you feel uneasy, you might be tempted to avoid it. Most of the things we put off eventually have to be done, and the anxiety we create as a result of procrastinating can be equal to or worse than the negative feelings we were trying to avoid.

The most common reason for procrastination is perfectionism. We tell ourselves that if we can't do it right, or *perfectly*, we'll put it off until we can. One of the more unusual reasons I've heard for procrastination comes from Mark Goulston, author of *Get Out Of Your Own Way*. His theory is that people procrastinate when they are lonely. We may not want to do something if we become isolated as a result. Therefore, enlisting the support of others or doing the dreaded task with someone else is often the solution. A procrastinator can become an activator when around others. That's why people have jogging buddies, study groups, and collaborators.

Take a good look at the things you tend to procrastinate. Identify the reasons you put off a particular task, and then try to come up with solutions to help you overcome procrastination.

For example, if you are postponing a project because it requires a large amount of time, blocking off time to do it will ensure you have the time you need to get it done. If you lack the information or resources you need, gathering what you'll need ahead of time will make it easier for you to do the task.

When faced with a large project, breaking it down into smaller tasks makes it less intimidating and more manageable. Being held accountable can be a motivator; announcing what you intend to do to friends, family, or coworkers might help, especially if they will be checking on your progress.

In addition to discovering the reasons you avoid certain tasks, determine what motivates you and reward yourself for doing something you didn't want to do. Although some people work better under the pressure of a deadline, doing so often creates additional stress for you and others.

When hurrying to meet a deadline, you leave little time to deal with unexpected problems and may become careless as you rush to finish. People have different work styles. If you tend to put your work off but share responsibilities with someone who prefers to get everything done ahead of time, you might find it challenging to work together.

When you have something you need to do, make a plan to meet the deadline. If you are overcommitted, speak up; it's better to address your concerns up front than to disappoint those who are counting on you to get something done.

Do it now, not later. Don't become a procrastinator. When you do, others will learn they can count on you. More important, you will be able to count on yourself.

TIP # 15
Under-promise and over-deliver.

You're young and you're working hard to build your career and a good reputation. You seek opportunities to demonstrate your ability, and you want other people to think highly of you. So when your boss asks if you'd like to do the research on meeting sites for the annual conference, you say yes. When she tells you she'd like you to present your findings at a meeting the following Monday morning, you tell her you will as you silently wonder how you'll manage to get it done.

Monday is just a week away and you've got other commitments to honor and deadlines to meet. You have classes almost every evening, and you are attending the wedding of a friend over the weekend. You're not sure how or when you'll get the research done, yet you say nothing. As a result, you stress-out and either do a poor job in your research or apologize for not being able to get it done. Either way, you've undermined your good intentions and disappointed your boss—and yourself.

No matter what excuse you give or how forgiving your boss appears, you both know you failed to deliver; you committed (made a promise) to do something, and you didn't do what you said you would. You took on the project with good intentions. You wanted to please your boss and prove your worth, but instead you let your boss down and diminished your value in her eyes.

Don't be too hard on yourself. Everyone over-commits at one time or another, and you're not likely to lose your job as a result of one mistake. Acknowledge your blunder and learn from your error. The next time you make another promise, be certain you can deliver. If you aren't sure you can get something done, say so. It's easier to work with realistic deadlines than it is to resolve the problems that arise from delays and unmet expectations.

If you try to please everyone, you'll end up pleasing no one. In fact, your desire to please will have the opposite effect; you will end up disappointing people, creating conflict, and damaging your reputation.

A sure way to avoid disappointment is by doing *more* than you promised. If you say you will call someone by the end of the week, don't wait until Friday at 5:00 P.M. (or worse yet, until

Monday) to call. Why not plan to get it done in advance? Can you imagine the surprise and delight on the other end of the phone when you call back *earlier* than expected? Every time you exceed expectations and over-deliver, you draw positive attention to yourself and make things easier for others.

Maybe you think you should never say "no" or "I can't" to your boss or turn down an exciting opportunity. "No" doesn't mean "never" and "I can't" doesn't mean "I won't." When you are forthright about what you can and cannot do, people will respect your honesty. When you *meet* expectations, people may not notice; after all, you're just doing your job. But people do notice when you fail to meet expectations and when you *exceed* them.

The next time you make a promise, *under-promise.* Set two dates: the date you promise *someone else* and the date you promise *yourself.* The date you set for yourself should be earlier than the one you give to someone else.

You'll reduce your stress, increase your productivity, and enhance your reputation. Few people manage to consistently over-deliver. Become one of the few who do.

TIP # 16
Don't sleep on the job.

What would you do if you became so tired you fell asleep at work in the midst of doing your job? How do you think your employer would react? Do you think he or she would:

- Wake you
- Reprimand you
- Send you home
- Fire you
- Praise you
- Allow you to sleep

Depending on where you live or work, any one of these answers could be right. Napping at work is the norm in some European countries, and a growing number of businesses elsewhere are providing nap rooms, allowing their employees to sleep on the job.

Don't get too excited, or too sleepy, just yet. When you're expected to be *working,* your employer won't be pleased to see you *sleeping.* If you are caught sleeping, you'll have some explaining to do, but if you are caught *slacking,* no excuse will do. Slackers cost companies billions of dollars.

There's a reason you get breaks and a reason you should take them, but try to use your work time for working, not for sleeping or slacking.

Five reasons you *shouldn't* sleep on the job:

- You're paid to work, not to sleep.

- Your snoring will disturb others.

- You have a big night planned and don't want to be too tired to enjoy it.

- You stayed up too late (and partied too much) the night before.

- You don't have anything else to do.

Five ways to *prevent* falling asleep on the job:

- Go to bed early and around the same time each night.

- Take breaks away from your desk.

- Get yourself moving. Go outside for a brief walk. Exercise regularly.

- Cut down your consumption of sugars, starches, and alcohol.

- Stand up, stretch, and take several deep cleansing breaths.

Five reasons to take a break to catch a nap:

- You can't stay awake.

- You're slurring your words (and the only drink you've had is coffee).

- You're making careless mistakes.

- You'll be more productive after a brief rest.

- You're falling asleep at your desk.

The *only* way to prevent slacking:

- Stay focused on your work!

TIP # 17

Ask questions; don't assume anything.

What should you do?

1. Your boss has given you an assignment, but you're not sure you understand it. Should you:

   A. Figure it out because you think you'll look stupid if you have to ask again

   B. Ask for clarification

   C. Go with your gut feeling

2. You make yourself hot chocolate in the company break room every morning. When you see someone drop change in the box on the counter, you wonder if you're supposed to be paying too. Should you:

   A. Keep using it for free

   B. Ask and find out

C. Pretend to put money in the box when others are around

3. Your supervisor tells you he didn't like the way you handled a phone call, but you're not sure what he didn't like. Should you:

A. Try to be nicer next time

B. Ask for specific reasons

C. Forget about it and hope it won't happen again

4. You'll be attending your first company holiday party. You know spouses are invited, but you're not married. You'd like to bring your significant other but don't know if you should. Should you:

A. Bring your significant other

B. Ask your manager if it's acceptable to bring your significant other.

C. Attend the party alone.

5. You've been working for the company just a few months. You hear about an opening in another department you'd like to apply for but wonder if it is the right thing to do. Should you:

A. Wait awhile to apply for another position

B. Ask someone in human resources

C. Apply for the position

6. Your reviews have been stellar, but you haven't had a raise in over a year, and you wonder when you can expect one. Should you:

A. Wait awhile and see

B. Ask your supervisor

C. Complain

7. You wonder if you can use the company computer over your break to check your personal e-mail. Should you:

   A. Use a coworker's computer

   B. Ask about policies

   C. Check your mail when no one is around to see you

8. You're not sure if you can wear sandals to work. Should you:

   A. Wear sandals

   B. Ask about dress code

   C. Leave them at home

9. Your deadline is approaching and you don't think you'll be able to meet it. Should you:

   A. Turn your project in a little late

   B. Ask the person expecting it

   C. Turn in what you've got done

The answer to all these questions is B. No question is dumb or too insignificant to ask. You are expected to ask questions as you learn. You are always better off asking than assuming.

Ask questions; don't assume anything.

Communication Skills

Achieve Effective Communication Through Body Language, Listening, Speaking, and Writing

TIP # 18
Turn off your cell phone.

I was speaking to a group of mothers and daughters and I was ready to bring my talk to a close. The moment I had been waiting for had arrived: I surprised my mother by asking her to join me onstage. I turned toward her and started to read the poem I had written about mothers and daughters. I could see tears filling the rims of my mother's eyes, and I felt a lump in the back of my throat. The room remained still, and the moment was rich with emotion, until it was abruptly interrupted by a ringing cell phone.

Everyone's attention shifted from the stage to the audience. People began chattering and snickering, and more than a few women pulled out purses to glance at their phones. By the time the excitement from the disturbance subsided, the poem I spent hours writing and the mood I worked so hard to create had evaporated. And although I tried, I never got the mood back.

It takes only one person, one phone, and one second to alter the tone of a meaningful experience, overshadowing the memory of a pivotal moment or important event. Sadly, my experience is not unique; cell phones have been responsible for disrupting funerals, weddings, and meetings and can be heard ringing in places of worship, hospitals, classrooms, restaurants, and more.

Even though announcements to "turn off your cell phone" are made and signs displayed, people bring their phones and forget or refuse to turn them off.

Convenience is the number-one reason people love their phones, according to a Cellmanners.com Internet poll. I love the convenience of my cell phone too. But when the fear of missing a call becomes so overwhelming I won't turn my phone off, I will fear my phone is controlling my every move.

Bring a cell phone to a job interview and it can prove disastrous; eighty-six percent of employers said they would automatically reject an otherwise qualified candidate who accepted a phone call during an interview according to a Vault.com poll. Cell phones are convenient, but if yours is hindering your progress or ringing in inappropriate places, it's time you consider leaving your cell phone at home.

Increase your chances of success, and decrease your chances of embarrassment.

TURN OFF YOUR CELL PHONE!

TIP # 19
Give yourself a voice over.

The first week the movie *Clueless* came out, I went with my daughters to see it. The main character, played by Alicia Silverstone, is a high school teenager who knows all about clothes, shoes, and cellular phones but is clueless about everything else. If you haven't seen the movie, consider watching it; you'll see a good example of how business people should *not* sound, and you'll get a good idea about dialect you should *avoid*. Silverstone's character sounds cute for a 16-year-old girl, but in a professional setting, sounding cute *isn't cute*.

Become aware of the jargon you use and the manner in which you speak. The way you talk may be the norm around your friends but might sound abnormal around other people.

Listen to people of *all* ages, and notice their manner of speech. What makes children *sound* like children? What makes teenagers *sound* like teens? Which teachers are easier to listen to, and which ones make you squirm or seethe? Do their statements sound like statements? Does their pitch go up or down? Do some people sound too squeaky or speak in monotone? Which styles of speech do you find most pleasing, and which styles are most frequently used?

Pay attention to your manner of speech, and make sure you communicate your thoughts to others clearly, concisely, and professionally. As you increase your awareness of speech patterns, be sure your statements sound like statements; you don't want to sound as if you are asking a question when you're not. *When you feel strongly about something, say it with confidence and sound as though you mean what you say.* "**I feel strongly about this.**" You're not seeking approval and you're not asking permission; you are making a *declaration*. Once you say it, *stop talking*.

When the tone of your voice goes *up* at the end of a sentence, instead of *down*, you undermine your intent and cause confusion for your listener. Instead of *making a declaration*, you *sound as though you're asking a question*.

When you make a statement that sounds like a question, you *sound unsure* of yourself, as if you need permission to feel the way you do. "I feel strongly? about this?" As a result of your "uptalk" (which comes from the higher tone at the end of your words and/or sentence), and your *lack of confidence* in your words (which comes from less emphasis on certain words), your listener interprets your statement this way: "I *think* I feel strongly, but I'm not really sure. Do *you* think it's *okay* if I do?"

There are other ways in which we undermine the intent of our conversations. Sometimes we use repetitive words or words that don't belong in a sentence at all. If you are asked why *you* are the best person for a job, be sure to answer clearly and concisely. Imagine an interviewer hearing this response:

"Well, I don't know, I mean, I think? I'd be really, really good? You know what I mean? Whatever, I really think? I'm really qualified? Like, I think? this would be a cool place to work and everything? Like, I work really hard, I catch on really fast, and like, I've got really good references and whatnot."

Give yourself a voice-over:

Get a clue. Pay attention to the way professional business people talk and sound.

Lower your pitch. The higher your pitch, the less appealing and more insecure you sound.

Turn up or down the volume. Speak up to be heard, but never so loudly you disturb other people.

Slow down. Take time to express your thoughts; slow down so people can understand you.

Watch your tone. If you say you are not upset but you sound irritated, your listener will assume you are irritated. The way you **sound** will overshadow the words you **say.**

Vary your inflection. You will sound more interesting when you do.

Emphasize the right words. Place emphasis where it belongs. If you have a point to make, emphasize your point.

TIP # 20
Drop the *um* and *ah; ya know what I mean?*

My daughter, Samantha, was eight years old and excited to share the events of her day. She was laughing and interrupting herself as she tried to get through the story she attempted to tell, and we were laughing along with her. When we realized how many times she kept using the word *okay*, listening to her tell the story became even funnier.

When I brought it to her attention and suggested she stop saying *okay* she agreed by saying, "Okay, I will." Every time I stopped her, she'd pause for a moment to collect her thoughts, and begin again. "Okay," she'd say, and then she'd laugh. "Okay, okay," and it happened again and again. The harder she tried, the more obvious it became; she wasn't okay without saying *okay*.

Samantha said *okay* when she needed some time to collect her thoughts. Instead of pausing in silence to think what to say next, she passed the time by saying *okay*. The next story she told, I counted 17 times she said *okay*. If you think reading this is frustrating, imagine listening to it!

Speech patterns are hard to break. When you are used to saying *um, ah*, or *okay*, you may not even realize you are saying those things. But other people do. They notice and it distracts them. When you use speech fillers repeatedly, other people can't help but notice. The problem is that it often becomes the *only* thing noticed, and the meaningful things you say get overlooked.

I remember a substitute teacher I had in high school. Her problem communicating her thoughts was so profound that I've never forgotten it. Her opening comments went something like this: "Um, today, um, I, um, need to, um, work with you, um, on the um, um, chapter, um, on um, um...." I don't remember anything else about the class, the teacher, or that day, but I do remember my impression and surprise at the number of *um*'s she said. I remember many of the students trying to hold back their laughter. For some, it was funny. For others, it was distracting and interfered with their ability to listen and understand what she was trying to say. For many, it was a source of irritation; her overuse of the word *um* made people feel uncomfortable. As I think about it now, I wonder if it might have been one of her first days teaching. She must have been nervous or terribly unprepared.

Being prepared is important. There will be times, however, when you are not as prepared as you'd like to be or caught off guard when you're asked a question. Whenever you're asked a question or having a conversation, you need time to process your thoughts and prepare your response.

No one wants to look dumb or seem unprepared, so when the pressure is on, we end up speaking when we have nothing to say. *Um*, *ah*, *er* are the *noises*, not the *words*, we mutter as we collect our thoughts and search for more effective words to say. Silence isn't as bad as you think. A pause here and there can be a welcome relief.

You may not be aware of the speech fillers you use or the frequency with which you use them. Become more aware of your speech. Ask your family and friends to become more aware too. When negative speech patterns are brought to your attention, you can replace them with different words or, if you'd prefer, with silent pauses.

You can improve your communication beginning today:

Use proper grammar. "Ya ain't gunna go nowhere when ya dunno nothin bout grammah."

Enunciate. Speak clearly; avoid garbled speech and mumbling.

Get rid of speech fillers. Minimize your use of the ums, ahs, ers, and okay's that take up space in your speech.

TIP # 21
Watch your tone when you're on the phone.

You can love it, you can hate it, and you might even be afraid of it, but you can't ignore it: The telephone is an important tool. In fact, of all the tools available, the telephone is one of the most influential in determining your overall effectiveness in your job search and work performance.

You might be more comfortable communicating by e-mail or in person, but there are times neither will do. E-mail can too easily be misconstrued and tends to feel impersonal. It isn't always possible to arrange a meeting to talk with someone face to face. Since it's most efficient to take care of matters as they arise, using the phone is often the most practical option.

When you know how to use the telephone effectively, you increase your comfort level, save time, and are better able to keep in touch with others. You may be thinking you already know how to use the telephone, but the *way* you use it is about to change. Your friends may not care how you sound on the phone, but when you call a potential employer or important client, it matters to the person on the other end. Your manner and tone will either help or hurt you, determining the way others respond to you. Every time you have a conversation with someone by phone, you validate, improve, or diminish the impression that person has about you.

A phone conversation is similar to any other type of conversation. If you had a face-to-face meeting with someone and the person you were physically with was working on the computer, glancing through mail, or carrying on another conversation instead of looking at you, how would you feel?

It's tempting to continue to work while you talk on the phone because you feel you are being more productive, but you are not accomplishing as much as you think. You're more likely to miss what you need to hear and overlook something you need to do. Ineffective communication can be costly. If you do not listen attentively to the person who is talking, your risk of misunderstanding increases dramatically. It's impossible to take notes while you're doing other things, and doing too many things at once leads to sloppy work and costly errors.

Although the person on the other end of the phone cannot see you, you are not as invisible as you think. Sound becomes amplified through the phone; if you are typing, chewing, or whispering, you *will* be heard. Act as you would if you were having a face-to-face conversation when you are on the phone.

- If you wouldn't walk in to someone's office and start talking without first making sure it was a good time, don't do it over the phone; always ask if it's a good time.

- If you wouldn't eat your lunch, clip your nails, or use the computer while talking with someone sitting across from you at your desk, don't do it during a telephone conversation.

- If you wouldn't have another conversation or answer your phone at the same time you were talking with someone else, don't do it when you're on the phone.

The person on the other end can't see you and cannot know if you are busy, in a hurry, or in a good mood or bad. You may be frustrated because your printer jammed, but if you *sound* frustrated, the person on the other end might think you are frustrated with him or her. Remember, they can *hear,* but they cannot *see,* so they'll fill in the blanks, right or wrong.

Put forth the extra effort to sound relaxed and cheerful when you're on the phone.

- *Smile* and you will put a smile in your voice; you will *sound* happy.

- *Stand* and you will become energized; you will *sound* energized.

- *Sit up* and you will think more clearly; you will *sound* focused.

- *Pay attention* and you will be attentive; you will *sound* interested.

Keep a mirror by your phone as a reminder that the person on the other end cannot see you, but your manner and tone can be seen and heard over the phone!

TIP # 22
Apologize; you can't always be right.

Apologize:

I'm sorry.

I apologize.

Please forgive me.

I am sorry I hurt you.

I beg your pardon.

I am so sorry.

Express your regret:

I wish I hadn't said that.

I feel terrible about this.

I regret what I did.

I'd do it differently if I could.

I regret hurting you.

I shouldn't have said that.

Take responsibility for your actions:

I am responsible; it's entirely my fault.

I overreacted.

I didn't pay attention.

I made a poor decision.

I was being defensive.

I wasn't careful enough.

Validate others:

You are right.

You didn't do anything wrong.

This isn't your fault.

You have a right to be upset

I'd be upset if I were you.

No one expects you to be perfect. Everyone makes mistakes. Admit yours when you make them. It doesn't matter which way you say it, as long as you sincerely mean it.

Apologize when appropriate; you can't always be right.

TIP # 23

Easy to use but can cause you to lose; use your phone to your advantage.

Meeting with someone in person is advantageous. Talking with someone face to face is the most personal and direct way to communicate. Seize opportunities to conduct interviews in person, meet clients in their offices, or discuss problems personally with other people. But when distance makes it too difficult or time constraints limit your options, the next best thing to a personal conversation is to talk over the phone.

Many of your initial conversations will occur over the phone. The person on the other end cannot see you, but you *will* be making an impression about yourself by your manner and the way you sound. Your ability to skillfully use the phone is crucial to your overall success. Learn to use it proficiently, and the phone will become one of your most valuable business tools.

It can be difficult reaching people directly and might take several calls before you speak with the person you want. You can always leave a message, but there's no guarantee it will be returned. Don't give up when you fail to reach someone, and don't avoid using the phone. The more you use it, the more comfortable and efficient you'll become.

From the moment you start sending out resumes, be prepared to receive calls on your phone. Your interview begins the *second* you, your voice mail, or anyone else answers your phone.

The people you call will respond favorably when you pay attention to the following:

- **Always have a specific purpose for your call.** Don't bother someone who's working on a critical deadline for an unimportant reason.

- **Identify yourself.** State your first and last name and company name, even when you think your voice will be recognized.

- **State the specific reason for your call at the *beginning* of the conversation.** This helps you stay focused and helps the person you called determine the relevance of your call.

- **Ask if it is a convenient time to talk.** Determine the best time to talk; it may be a convenient time for you but might not be for the other person.

- **Keep your conversation brief.** Focus on your main objective, and say good-bye when you accomplish what you intended; don't waste time—yours or anyone else's.

- **Leave an informative message.** Speak *clearly*, *s-l-o-w-l-y*, and *repeat your name and number*, both at the beginning and end of your message. There's nothing more frustrating than having to replay a message over and over in an attempt to understand it or capture the phone number to call back.

- **Request a specific response.** Tell the person what you expect. If you need a response, tell the person *what* you need and *when* you need it.

The people calling you will respond favorably when you pay attention to the following:

- **Answer your phone promptly.** Always answer your phone and set your voice mail to pick up by the third ring.

- **Identify yourself.** Include your name and company name in your greeting.

- **Keep your voice mail greeting brief.** State your first and last name and your company's name, as well as when the caller can expect a return call; if you won't be calling back as soon as you can, don't say you will.

- **Maintain a current voice mail greeting.** Hearing you say "Happy Holidays" is nice around the holidays but irritating soon after. Informing callers you are on vacation long after you're back is a disservice.

- **If you change your greeting daily, *change it daily*.** It's pointless to hear about your schedule for September when it's the third week of October. The *silent* message of an outdated greeting suggests you are overwhelmed and too busy to change it or too careless to remember.

- **Give the person on the other end your full attention.** Anything you do has the probability of being heard. If you can't stop typing, writing, or talking with someone else, admit it isn't a good time to talk.

Additional ways to make a good impression over the phone:

- When you place someone on hold, use the hold button; don't put your hand over the receiver or put the phone down and leave it.

- Limit the time you keep someone on hold; check back after 30 seconds and thank them for holding.

Return calls promptly, ideally within one business day.

Eliminate background noise and distractions; turn down the sound on your computer, music playing, or other interferences.

Don't eat, chew gum, or smoke while on the phone.

Listen attentively; don't interrupt.

Talk directly into the receiver.

If you don't have a good reason to make a call, don't make it.

TIP # 24
Emailmatters@work; don't leave a trail of bad e-mail.

Your image is important in person, on the phone, on paper, and electronically. Spend your time at work doing work; don't surf the Internet or e-mail friends and family. There's a good chance your company is monitoring your computer. This means that the trail of e-mails you send or receive, and every Web site you visit, will be followed and found. Don't risk your job or reputation. Follow the basic rules of e-mail etiquette.

A few precautions:

Don't hide behind e-mail. E-mail isn't always the best vehicle for communication. If you use e-mail to avoid phone calls or meetings, be careful. E-mail can be impersonal. Balance your use of e-mail with other channels of communication.

Save the address for last. Do not address an e-mail until you are ready to send it; this will prevent you from accidentally sending it before you are finished.

Save your e-mails. You may want to access the information some time in the future.

Think twice before you hit send. Don't send an e-mail when you are upset. If you are not sure about sending it, don't.

Send a hard copy. When you send something of importance, send a hard copy via mail or personal delivery, too.

To add warmth and make a good impression:

Change your e-mail name. Use a professional screen name. The name you've been using is fine for your friends, but "eyemhot" or "2kool4u" on a resume won't help your job-search image, and it could hurt it.

Be discreet with e-mail. No e-mail is private. If you'd be embarrassed to have anyone else see it, don't send it.

Begin and end with a greeting. If you wouldn't begin a phone call without saying hello or end it without saying good-bye, don't do it in e-mail.

Watch your tone. Don't use all uppercase letters; it's the equivalent of shouting and you'll come on too strong. Don't use all lowercase letters; it's the equivalent of whispering and you'll appear too timid.

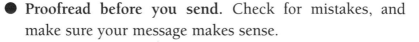

Proofread before you send. Check for mistakes, and make sure your message makes sense.

Don't send a message you should convey personally instead. Don't use e-mail because it's easier for you. When it's too personal or sensitive to send in a message, deliver the news by phone or in person.

To ensure your e-mails will be read:

Be brief. The shorter the e-mail, the more likely it will be read.

Use the subject line. If you don't include a subject, it may never get opened.

Write an informative subject line. Your subject line should state the purpose of the e-mail, any deadlines, and action required. Example: *Request for employee nominations due by June 1.*

Be concise. State your purpose for writing up front; then stick to your purpose.

To increase your chances of a prompt response:

Inform the recipient when you send an attachment. Even though it will show up, mention it in your e-mail, or it could be overlooked.

Call when sending time-sensitive mail. Don't depend on e-mail. If you want to be sure something gets read, call and tell the recipient to look for it.

Include contact information. Make it easy for people to contact you. Use a signature with your name, company name, and phone number. Your snail mail address is optional.

Be specific. Tell your reader what to do. If you need a response by Friday at noon, say so. If you are requesting a meeting, specify when you need a response. If you are sending information and don't need a response, tell your reader.

Reference previous e-mail. If you are responding to a previous e-mail, mention it in your subject line.

To send professional-looking e-mail:

Use spell-check. Mistakes reflect poorly on you. Use spell-check, but don't rely on it; some words might get overlooked.

● Write in complete sentences. Don't take shortcuts. Sending *Okay* as a reply is unacceptable.

Use proper punctuation. Punctuate your e-mail as you would punctuate any other document.

Write out complete words. Don't abbreviate words; spell them out.

Stick with words. Don't use clip art, smiley faces, or emoticons.

Use professional language. Don't use slang, jargon, or profanity.

Create a new document. Don't continue to reply to an e-mail that's been going back and forth for months. Ideally, you should create a new e-mail every time you write one or at least after the second or third round of sending an e-mail back and forth.

Avoid fancy stationery. If you use stationery, keep it subtle; avoid anything too colorful or distracting.

Be considerate of others:

Don't send jokes or forward chain letters. We all have plenty of e-mail already; don't add to the overload.

Be polite. Say *please* and *thank you* when making a request or when someone does something nice for you.

Don't critique someone's e-mail. There's no need to point out errors or mistakes you discover in someone else's document.

Limit the number of attachments. Attachments carry viruses; be careful what you open and send.

Inquire about policies. Some companies don't allow employees to open attachments. Know the policies before you send and receive.

TIP # 25
Say what you mean and mean what you say.

Say what you mean and mean what you say; don't say what you
don't mean to say.

When you say it, you should mean it; don't let fear get in your
way.

Don't say what you *think* you're *supposed* to say; say what you
mean to say.

It's easy to handle the truth; it's the lies that get in the way.

When you say what someone *wants* you to say, you don't say
what *you* want to say.

People ask your opinion to hear it; so say what you need to say.

Don't tell me your plans to do it if you won't be following
through.

If you make a mistake, admit it; it's okay if I hear it from you.

Once your words leave your mouth, you can't get them back;
they travel only one way.

Be careful how you use your words; *say what you mean and
mean what you say.*

How clearly do you think you communicate? Most people
could improve their communication, yet *think* they communicate
effectively. Do you think you say what you mean and mean what
you say? See for yourself:

● Do you ever *pad* the truth to avoid hurting someone?

If you do, you'll end up hurting people when they find out.
Padding the truth is equivalent to lying.

● Do you ever tell people what you think they want to hear?

When people ask you a question, they want to hear what *you* think. When you shade the truth, *you're not telling the truth.*

● Do you ever say yes instead of no or no instead of yes to avoid making someone mad?

If you do, you're likely to get mad at *yourself* when you find yourself doing something you'd rather not. When you say anything other than the truth, *you are telling a lie.*

● Do you ever tell only part of the story?

Maybe you think it is easier for your listener, so you leave out some of the facts. Maybe you want to prevent someone from getting mad or from making yourself look bad. Whatever your reason, when you tell only part of the story, *you are* not *telling the truth.*

● Do you say you'll do something but fail to follow through?

When you say you will do something, others assume you'll do it. Maybe you meant "if time permits"; maybe you meant "you'll try." But if what you meant isn't what you said, *you have told a lie.*

Communication doesn't have to be complicated. Speak the truth. Don't pad it; soften it or cover it. *Say what you mean and mean what you say!*

TIP # 26
Power up your presentation skills.

My oldest daughter, Stephanie, was selecting her classes for the second semester. When I suggested she take a speech class, she resisted. "I don't like making speeches; I get nervous when I have to talk in front of people. My face turns red and it's embarrassing."

I tried to convince her to take the class and assured her it would help reduce her nervousness, but I couldn't promise her face would never turn red. I did, however, tell her it probably wouldn't turn *as red* as a result of the practice and confidence she'd gain from taking the class. After wavering, Stephanie decided to take the class. And although it took her awhile to tell me, she said that she was glad she did.

Few things generate as much anxiety as speaking in front of other people. Fear of embarrassment is one of the most common reasons. Giving into that fear is a mistake, because few things are as important to your career as your ability to communicate your knowledge, thoughts, and ideas.

You will be asked to present information numerous times throughout your career. At times you will present information in your office in front of only one or two people or in a meeting with three, four, or more. On other occasions you might be asked to present to a very large group. Whether you are responding to an impromptu request or delivering a planned presentation, you'll want to make a powerful presentation.

I've discovered that doing the thing you fear helps rid you of fear. If you fear presentations or speaking to a group (which most people do), you may never eliminate your fear entirely, but I can assure you if you prepare in advance and practice every chance you get, you'll become much more comfortable.

Nervousness has its advantages. You can't ignore the physical symptoms you feel, so do what you can to eliminate them—practice and prepare! Some of your favorite athletes and performers say they get nervous too, often before a performance. It doesn't *stop* them from performing; it *helps* them *get ready* to perform.

Ten steps to help you power up your presentation skills:

1. **Identify your objectives.** Why have you been asked to present? What do you need to accomplish?

2. **Know your topic.** Become an expert; gather as much information as you can about the topic you will be addressing.

3. **Know your audience.** Find out who will be attending, and learn all you can about them; what do they want and need to take away from your presentation?

4. **Develop your message.** Avoid information overload; identify your most important points, and select the information that best supports them. Get rid of the fluff and stick with the most relevant and critical information you have.

5. **Organize your ideas.** An effective presentation has a beginning (*tell them what you plan to tell them*), middle (*tell them what you need to tell them*), and end (*tell them what you've told them*).

6. **Substantiate your message.** The burden of proof is on you. Verify your facts and data, and validate each point you make. Support your message by selecting and including various studies, surveys, statistics, stories, examples, or other relevant information.

7. **Include visual aids.** As you *tell* your audience what you want to tell them, *show* them the information as well. Most people find it difficult to listen attentively for extended periods of time. Visual aids add variety and make your presentation more interesting. However, don't depend entirely on your PowerPoint or other visuals. Always have a back-up plan should you run into problems with equipment.

8. **Prepare in advance.** Practice and preparation are the keys to reducing stress and anxiety. Practice in front of other people, in front of a mirror, or when you're alone in your room or car. Never memorize your talk or read your entire presentation word for word from a piece of paper. Prepare brief notes on numbered note cards instead.

9. **Engage your audience.** Ask for and respond to questions, and always speak directly to your audience. Make

eye contact, smile, and stand up straight. Keep your hands *out of* your pockets so you can use them as you speak. When you feel comfortable, your audience will feel comfortable. They *want* you to succeed.

10. **End on time.** If your presentation is supposed to be over at 10:00 A.M., end by then. Unless you've been given permission or have prepared your audience in advance, the *minute* you are scheduled to stop speaking, your audience expects you to **stop**. If you don't, your audience *will*; they will disconnect and stop listening to you.

TIP # 27
Please and *thank you* are powerful words.

You can use them *anytime* you want.

You can use them *anywhere* you want.

You can use them when you *want* something.

You can use them when you *get* something.

You can use them with anyone.

You can share them with everyone.

They will make people *feel* good.

They will make you *look* good.

You will appear nicer when you use them.

They will further your relationships.

They will improve your image.

They will help you gain cooperation.

They will boost morale.

They will humble you.

They will help you.

They cannot be bought.

They cannot be sold.

They never go out of style.

They never get old.

What are they?

They are three very *powerful* words: *Please* and *thank you.* It's up to you to use them.

TIP # 28
Expand your vocabulary.

Have you ever stalled for time as you struggled to express a thought or search for the right words to use? Have you ever had trouble understanding the words you heard others use? The ability to articulate a thought and communicate it clearly is important to every aspect of your life. Ineffective communication leads to breakdowns in communication, misunderstandings, and costly errors. Communication skills are critical to your professional success.

The depth and breadth of your vocabulary influences your ability to communicate effectively. Most successful professionals possess advanced vocabulary skills, yet most recent graduates haven't actively attempted to improve their vocabularies since high school, according to Greg Ragland, Vice President of Marketing for The Executive Vocabulary Program.

In his workshops, Ragland encourages attendees to reactivate their interest and awareness of new words. He recommends keeping a vocabulary journal, writing down new words and how they are used whenever you hear them. This will help you understand the context in which they are used at work. You will benefit by understanding and using the same words your colleagues use.

Don't try to impress people by using big words you can't pronounce or don't understand; you don't want to appear as though you don't know what you're talking about or sound unnatural. When you expand your vocabulary, you expand your knowledge. Pay attention to new words you *read* and new words you *hear*. People judge you by the words you use. Build your vocabulary and build your confidence, one word at a time.

TIP # 29
Master the art of SMALL TALK.

S **tart a conversation.**
You're not the only one who feels awkward at social events. It's no fun to stand alone while everyone else is talking and having fun. If you're waiting for someone to start a conversation with you, stop waiting and start talking, and move away from the corner as you do. Get out of your seat and away from the wall. It's easier than you think.

M **ake people feel comfortable.**
If you want people to enjoy talking with you, they need to feel comfortable being around you. If you are at an event and see someone standing or sitting alone, walk over and introduce yourself and invite him or her to sit with you. Shake hands with the people you meet, and introduce them to people they do not know. Make people feel comfortable, and you'll be welcome wherever you go.

A **sk questions.**
You don't have to tell funny jokes, interesting stories, or say much of anything at all. When you open your mouth, ask an open-ended question and watch the

conversation evolve. "How did you get into this line of work?" is open-ended and will help people open up to you. It's better than "Do you like working here?" because someone could give you a yes or no response and the conversation could stop right there.

L ead the conversation.

Lead conversations *away* from sex, politics, religion, income, and personal ailments. Lead the conversation with the safest small talk topics. The weather, sports, current events, industry-related trends or news, hobbies, and movies will get you off to a good start.

L isten attentively.

Be a good listener; pay attention to what's being said, remember names, and look directly at the person talking. Don't let your eyes wander or try to listen in on another conversation. When you listen attentively, you silently let other people know you care.

T ry to keep it positive.

There are plenty of things to complain about. There's turmoil in the world and there's natural disasters. There are diseases with no cure and too few second chances. Relationships are challenging, and work can be a pain, but when you're making small talk, it isn't the time to complain. Small talk is meant to be small; don't waste time trying to solve problems, debate controversial issues, or discuss the woes of the world. Keep it upbeat and positive. It's meant to be kept small.

A ppear interested.

You don't have to talk a lot to be considered interesting. When you appear interested in others, they'll become interested in you. Don't worry about what to say. The conversation shouldn't revolve around *you*. When you get people talking, you take the pressure off, and they will think highly of you.

L ink the conversation.

The best conversations are those that link two people, enabling a bond to be formed. Discovering you have a mutual acquaintance, enjoy the same hobby, share a love of animals, and anything else you find you have in common will put you both on common ground. Even the smallest commonalities can link one person to another. Look for links, and you'll form stronger bonds.

K eep it moving.

Think of a conversation as a game. Imagine an invisible ball being passed back and forth throughout your conversation. You'll have the ball when you start a conversation, but you'll want to quickly pass it to your partner. When you have the ball, it is your turn to talk, but never hold on to the ball too long. The winner of the game is the one who does the best job of giving the ball away. If you monopolize the ball, you'll slow the momentum of the game. The more you practice, the better you will play. Just remember to keep the ball (and the conversation) moving.

TIP # 30
"Sit still!" "Stand up straight!" *Pay attention to your body language.*

"Sit still." "Stand up straight." "Look at me when I'm talking to you." You've probably heard these and similar remarks before. They may be irritating to hear at the time, but there's a good reason the adults in your life issue these commands. They want to help you *pay attention* to your body language. Since the day you were born, you've been communicating with your body; your parents knew you were happy when you'd smile and needed no words for reinforcement.

Even as an adult, people can tell when you're happy. Everything you do sends a message. You walk fast when you're in a hurry, and you slow down when you're relaxed. You pay attention when you're interested, and you look away when you are not. You stand tall when you feel proud and slump your shoulders when you're down. People who don't know you can tell a lot about you just by looking at you. You can try to hide your feelings, but your body language is too revealing.

What language does your *body* speak? Your body language speaks loudly and clearly to others and at times may conflict with your words. When you say something verbally, but communicate something else visually, you confuse people. In an attempt to understand your message, people will look for ways to understand what you are trying to say. They may want to believe your words (your intent) but are influenced more by your actions (your response). We pick up on the visual clues we see, putting out trust in the things we *see* over the things we *hear.*

When your words and your body are in conflict, your *body* will always win.

If you *tell* your friend you don't mind waiting but *become* impatient while you wait, your friend will think you are impatient.

If you *say* you are interested in a job but *look* uninterested during the interview, the interviewer will think you are not interested.

If you *say* you're not nervous but *appear* anxious, people will question your confidence.

Powerful people *give the impression* they are powerful and know how to command attention. They use their posture, expressions, gestures, and eyes to communicate powerfully and effectively.

They weren't born this way; they've worked at and perfected the language their bodies speak.

Powerful ways to command attention:

● Stand, sit, and walk straight and tall.

● Hold your head high.

● Look at people directly—make eye contact.

● Slow down.

● Be still.

● Control your gestures.

● Smile.

● Tilt your head.

● Nod.

● Vary your expressions; show your happiness, interest, and compassion for others.

You don't have to *feel* calm to project coolness or wait years to gain the confidence you need. The next time you feel unsure of yourself, *act as if* you feel assured. People believe what they see. If you want to become a confident, powerful person, use your body language to help you. You can be whoever you want to be.

TIP # 31

If you wouldn't say it to someone's face, don't say it.

Your ability to get along with people is important. So is your ability to adapt to the different types of people you meet.

The relationship component of a job can be crucial. If your friendships are strong and you feel you belong, they enhance your overall work experience. If you feel left out or alone and have conflicts with others, however, it can make going to work every-day feel like a chore. If you never figured out how to deal with the troublemakers in your life before or how to get along in a group, you may find yourself facing some of the same issues you've struggled with in the past. But if someone annoys you, discredits you, or spreads rumors about you, you don't have to respond as you did before; you can choose a new way to respond.

If someone you work with becomes a nuisance, what will you do?

If someone is spreading rumors about you, what will you do?

If you see the supervisor you loathe at a bar with someone other than his wife, will you remain silent or tell your friends at work?

If you can't stand the smell of your coworker's aftershave or the way he smacks his lips when he chews, will you tell him? Will you tell others about him?

The office grapevine is alive and well; gossip is just as prevalent at work as it was in school and it is not easy to ignore. You can pay attention to it and learn from it, but be careful about adding to it. Spreading rumors and gossip about other people can damage reputations and hurt relationships. Having something said *about* you often hurts more than something that is said *to* you.

The next time you're ready to say something you shouldn't or if what you are about to say could hurt someone, think twice. If you wouldn't say it to someone's face, don't say it; you'll sleep better at night.

Build trust. If someone tells you something in confidence, keep it to yourself.

Be direct. If you have a problem with someone, speak directly with that person.

Get to the source. If someone has been talking about you, don't talk about them or what they say to everyone else; go directly to the source of your problem.

Avoid spreading gossip. Don't spread rumors; be the roadblock where rumors stop.

Don't talk about other people. Steer your conversations away from talk about other people and toward something of greater value.

Speak well of colleagues. If you want to say something about someone, think of something positive to say.

Remain silent. If you don't have anything nice to say, don't say anything at all. You've heard this before. Now's the time to apply it.

TIP # 32
Always send a thank-you note.

Have you ever thought about the way you go about opening your mail? Which pieces do you automatically throw in the trash, which ones do you put aside to open later, and which ones do you select to open first? Is it the bills, the solicitations, or the personal mail you receive that gets your attention?

Did you know that most people, whether they are aware of it or not, open personalized, hand-addressed envelopes first? We don't receive personalized mail everyday, so we tend to appreciate it when we do.

You probably prefer to say "thanks" or "happy birthday" with e-mail; after all, it's cheaper and less time consuming. But when you send a personal message through an electronic greeting, you're also sending a less personal message. E-mail is less personal; there's no envelope to open and no card or note to display, and there's a chance it might never get opened at all or opened after the intended day.

Whenever someone does something nice for you, do something nice in return; *show your appreciation.* Don't count on a call, an e-mail, or "hey thanks" the next time you see the person. Put your pen to paper and use the most effective (and impressive) way to say "thanks."

The busier you are, the more difficult it is to stay in touch with family and friends. Without the day-to-day connection that comes from living, working, or going to school together, you'll have to make an effort to keep in touch. E-mails and phone calls are fine, but on special occasions, make them more special by sending a card or small gift.

Celebrate the events of the important people in your life, and not just at holiday time. Send birthday cards, anniversary cards, and congratulations cards, too. You'll make someone's day when you do.

Show your support and happiness for others. By sending a card, take the time to *personally* acknowledge someone who gets married, has a baby, or is promoted. Be there for people in good and bad times. Send sympathy cards to people who are grieving and notes of encouragement to those who are ill. You will never know the impact sending a note or a card will have. People need other people, and knowing you care will make a difference.

If you want people to do nice things for you, do nice things for other people. Keep in touch, remember life's important events, and whenever someone does something nice (including interviewing you), *show your appreciation; send a thank-you note.*

TIP # 33
Remember this f—r letter word—*DON'T!*

You're stuck in traffic on your way to an important meeting. You try to call your office, but you can't get through because your cell phone battery is dead. When you finally arrive, you discover your coworker has taken full credit for a project you worked on together. When you look for the spreadsheet you need to prove your involvement, it's nowhere to be found. As you shuffle your papers and look through your folders, you knock over your cup of coffee. The coffee is everywhere: on your pants, on your papers, and on the conference room table and floor. When you access your computer for the spreadsheet you need, it isn't there.

We all have days when everything seems to go wrong and times we deal with more than our fair share of stress. When you're alone in your car, you can respond anyway you choose. If your cell phone goes dead, you can throw it, and you can swear at it; no one cares if you do. But when you are around other people at work and you lose your cool, you'll lose their respect along with it.

When you overreact, use expletives, or storm out of a room, you draw negative attention to yourself. Your family and friends might put up with your outbursts, but your employers, coworkers, and clients will not.

If you think some swear words are worse than others, you're probably right. In a business environment, however, there are no varying degrees of profanity; swearing is swearing.

Don't ever swear. *Don't* offend others. *Don't* discredit yourself. *Don't* lose control.

The next time you are about to let a bad word slip out of your mouth, stop, catch your breath, and remember this important word of advice: *DON'T!*

TIP # 34
Listen.

When you hear, you need to listen.

When you listen, you pay attention; when you pay attention, you stop talking.

When you stop talking, you engage; when you engage, you feel connected.

When you feel connected, you invest; when you invest, you see value.

When you see value, you commit; when you commit, you resolve.

When you resolve, you truly focus; when you focus, you can learn.

When you learn, you gain knowledge; when you gain knowledge, you will grow.

When you grow, you will improve; when you improve, you can advance.

When you advance, you develop; when you develop, you mature.

When you mature, you start to notice; when you notice, you can see.

When you can see, you understand; when you understand, you grasp the concept.

When you grasp the concept, you have communication.

When you have communication, you have cooperation.

When you have cooperation, you can achieve anything.

So Listen!

Improve your listening skills by remembering to *stop, look,* and *listen.*

When someone is speaking to you:

STOP what you are doing. Stop talking. Stop to hear what someone's saying.

LOOK at the person speaking to you. Look interested. Look and see a different point of view.

LISTEN and you will learn. Listen and you will understand. Listen and you will hear.

Leadership Skills

Become a Leader

TIP # 35

Lead by example.

When you think of people you consider strong leaders, who comes to mind? Do you think of well-known individuals in high-level leadership positions in business, entertainment, or sports? Do you think of world or political leaders?

Many people look up to those with fame, fortune, or status and assume these things signify a good leader. But sometimes these things create a false sense of leadership. A true leader doesn't thrive or rely on power, control, affluence, or name recognition. Although many successful leaders have these things, plenty of successful leaders do not.

You don't have to be the person in charge to be an effective leader. Natural leaders earn respect as a result of what they *do*, not because of who they are. The best leaders *lead by example*.

Think about the leaders who have been a positive influence in *your* life. Is there a special teacher, family member, neighbor, friend, or other role model who's helped guide you? Think about the people you respect, those you turn to for advice. Is there someone you look up to, enjoy listening to, or someone who enjoys listening to *you?* Is there anyone who motivates you to try harder, be better, or take a risk?

The leaders capable of leading *you* are not necessarily those who are in the spotlight. Be sure you don't overlook the leaders in *your* life—the people who've taken time to talk with you and help you.

There are renowned leaders who do great things and earn the praise and honor they get. There are also leaders we rarely, if ever, read or hear about who deserve but may not ever get the recognition and appreciation they've earned. Some people lead quietly and discreetly. They create and inspire change in others. They don't live spectacular lives. They don't consider themselves to be great leaders and may not even realize they are making a difference. They simply lead by being who they are.

If you think you're too young to lead others, think again. Your actions inform others about who and what is important to you. Your words encourage, or discourage, others. You guide and influence people every day whether you do it intentionally or not. Are you being the kind of leader you want to be?

You determine what you say; you determine what you do. Actions speak louder than words; do your actions speak well of you? When you say you'll do something, *do you do it?*

Your words have more impact than you think—think about the things that you say. If you don't have something nice to say, *don't say it*. If you're afraid you might say something you'll regret, *don't say it*. If it's negative, judgmental, or critical, *don't say it*.

Treat people as you wish to be treated. Strive to be your best and bring out the best in others. Live and lead your life purposefully, carefully, and intentionally, and you will lead others to do the same. Lead by example.

TIP # 36

Be a lifelong learner.

Once you've met the requirements for graduation, your formal education will be complete. You should be proud of yourself and the work you've done. If you're finished with school for now, you can put away your backpack and stop worrying about your grades. You're not a student anymore, but whether you know it or not, in many ways your education has just begun.

Learning is a lifelong process. Many things can't be taught in a classroom, and some of your most valuable life lessons lie ahead of you. You've got a lot of living and learning to do. Continue your education and become a student of life.

As your life changes, so will you. Your learning curve will be highest anytime you do something new or make a major change. When you move away from home or to another city, you will become more independent and responsible. If you are involved in a long-term relationship, marry, or have children, you will learn even more about yourself and others. If you become a student of life, you will learn something new every day.

Continuing your education doesn't mean you have to continue to go to school or take night classes. It is up to you, however, to develop new skills and expand your knowledge. Make sure you keep up with current trends. Take advantage of opportunities to add to your credentials. Consider specializing in a chosen field. Even if you never considered yourself to be a good student or didn't care about learning before, you might be surprised to discover how much you enjoy learning when you're interested in a given subject.

Learn from your mistakes. Some of the lessons you learn will be subtle and accumulative, others immediate and profound. You will learn when you succeed, and you will learn when you fail. Don't be afraid of making a mistake or become embarrassed when you do. Give yourself credit for trying. Everyone makes mistakes. Make mistakes and learn from them. It's one of the most effective ways to learn.

Learn from others. You don't have to learn everything on your own or learn the hard way. There is a wealth of information out there, and more people than you realize are happy to help you. Don't be too proud to ask for help or advice. As long as you ask after you've done some research yourself and aren't taking the easy way out, you will flatter those you ask for advice. Expand your network to learn from others. Join the organizations and associations in your field. Learn from the meetings you attend and learn from the people you meet. The wider your network and the more frequently you talk with others, the more knowledge you will gain.

Learn by acquiring new knowledge and skills. Read professional journals, read books, read the newspaper, stay on top of industry trends, and know public information about your company and its competitors. Never stop acquiring knowledge. The more you know, the more value you bring to everything you do.

Learn by doing. Experience really is the best teacher. Overcoming fear is empowering; face your fears. Stop thinking about what you want to do and start doing something now. Every risk you take will make you stronger, wiser, and teach you something new.

Life is an education; become a student of life. There is much for you to learn about life and from life. The classroom is always open and there is more information than ever before. Commit to your ongoing education. Be a lifelong learner.

TIP # 37
You don't get what you want; you get what you ask for.

It's important to think about your future and determine what you want. The more you focus on a goal, the more likely you are to accomplish it. Some goals are so personal you may chose to keep them to yourself. It is difficult, however, to accomplish everything alone. The more you talk about your goals, the more real they become. Don't keep your dreams to yourself. If no one knows what you want, no one will be able to help you.

Jan was so upset when she discovered that someone else received the promotion she wanted that she quit her job. When she gave her notice, she hoped her manager would beg her to stay, but he did not. Jan did not get the promotion she wanted and left a job she loved because she had her heart set on something she never told anyone about, including the manager doing the hiring. She assumed others knew what she needed and wanted. How could anyone know when she kept it all to herself? Did she expect others to read her mind?

Most people are too busy dealing with their own issues and problems to worry about everyone else. If you want something, don't hide the truth, drop hints, or expect others to read your mind.

Speak up. No one will ever know what you want unless you say what it is. If there's something you want, whether it's a promotion, more money, or a favor from a friend, talk about it. Don't keep it a secret, and don't expect others to know what you want unless you tell them. Talk to the people who make the decisions—talk to those who can help you. No one will hear you unless you speak up. Tell people what you need and ask for what you want.

Be specific. Be specific about your requirements and expectations. Don't rely on others to speak for you. People can't fill in the blanks. It won't do you any good to hope for what you want if no one knows what you're hoping for.

Be realistic. People will take you seriously only if your requests are reasonable and realistic. Outlandish requests can't be fulfilled. Don't ask someone for something impossible. Make it easy for others to honor your request.

Be honest. If you're asked for your opinion, give your opinion. You don't have to agree with everyone else. Be frank about your point of view without being argumentative or alienating others. You need a better response than "I don't know" or "I don't care." It's okay if you have a different perspective as long as you're honest about the way you feel.

Be accountable. If you want something, it's up to you to get it. Be responsible for what you do and say.

Be direct. Don't make demands; make reasonable requests. Determine what you want. Then go directly to the person with the authority to honor your request. You will earn respect for knowing and stating what you want and will improve your standing with others.

Your future is up to you. Let others know what you need. There's no guarantee you'll get what you ask for, but you will increase your chances.

TIP # 38
Follow your heart.

When it was time for Colleen to declare a major, she wasn't sure what to do. The subjects she enjoyed most were those people told her she couldn't do anything with professionally. Under pressure to find a career, she declared accounting as her major after doing well in the accounting class she took.

At times she wondered if she had made a mistake, but she pushed her concerns away and stuck with her decision. After graduation, Colleen got a job with a large accounting firm. She was compensated well and her success made her the envy of her peers, but she remained dissatisfied. Although she did well at her job, she didn't really like working in accounting.

Whenever she mentioned her frustration to family or friends, they told her she would be crazy to give up such a great job and career. Assuming they knew what was best for her, she listened to their advice instead of listening to herself and following her heart.

After working at a job she loathed for seven years, Colleen's physical and emotional health began to deteriorate. She suffered severe anxiety attacks and could no longer ignore the circumstances that were affecting her health and well-being. Her idea of success didn't match what others told her success was.

It took some time, but when she finally paid attention to her heart instead of her pocket book, she quit her job, took a different one in a public relations firm, and went back to school. As a result, her health and her peace of mind improved.

Colleen knew all along what was best for her, but instead of following her heart, she followed the advice of others. Look inward, not outward, to find the answers to your most important questions. No one knows better than you what's best for you.

Consider carefully the advice that others give you; pay more attention to the advice you give to yourself. Use your head, but don't ignore how you feel. Sometimes you just *know*. Some feelings are too difficult to explain, especially to others who have difficulty listening to their hearts.

When your head and your heart tell you two different things, carefully consider your choices. Look at all sides, the risks, and consequences. If your feelings are stronger than what you *think* is right, get out of your head and follow your heart.

TIP # 39

Do the work you love and love the work you do.

Whether you work full or part time, you will spend more time at work than almost anywhere else. Are you willing to spend the majority of your time (and your life) working at a job you dislike, or do you want to spend your time doing something you enjoy?

When you enjoy the work you do, it won't feel like work at all. You will feel, and know, that you're doing the work you were meant to do. Don't worry if you're not sure what you're meant to do just yet. It can take time to figure it out.

Pay attention. Pay attention to your activities, both in and outside of work. Notice what you are doing when you feel most energized and alert. Which tasks do you enjoy doing most and which the least? Can you detect a lifelong pattern, or are you establishing new interests and habits?

Find your passion. If you could spend your time doing anything you wanted, what would you do? If money wasn't an issue, would your answer change? If you had so much money you could give some away, who would you give it to? Think about your interests. What are your favorite things to do? What subjects interest you most? What topics are you inclined to talk about, think about, or read about? Do you have a talent or skill you'd like to improve? The answers to these questions can help guide you. Start by identifying the things you are most interested in or most enthusiastic about. Your interests and enthusiasm indicate your passion.

Look for meaning in your work. If getting a paycheck is the only thing motivating you to get out of bed and go to your job each day, you need to find more meaning in your work. Look beyond your compensation; look for something you can give. Can a coworker use your help? Can you make a client smile? Can you find a way to challenge yourself? The more meaningful your work is to you and others, the more satisfied you will be doing it.

Do more than get by. Are you arriving at work each day eager to do a good job? If you show up physically but are absent emotionally, *you* aren't showing up for work at all; only your body is. If you are getting by and doing the bare minimum, it won't be too long before you say good-bye to your job. There are plenty of bodies for hire but too few outstanding employees.

Don't let your job define you. You are not your job, but when you love your job it will be a *part* of who you are. Some people lose themselves in their work. Work shouldn't be an escape from life but a part of life. It's important to get good feelings from your job, but make sure you get good feelings other places as well. Work hard at work, but work hard at your outside relationships and hobbies too.

Money isn't everything. Money can buy you many things, but one thing is certain: Money will *not* buy you happiness. A study that appeared in the *Journal of Personality and Social Psychology*, published by the American Psychological Association, put money at the bottom of the list of the psychological needs that bring happiness and fulfillment. Self-esteem, competence, and a feeling of closeness with others were at the top of the list.

Some people love every job they have, not because each job is ideal but because they find the good in what they do. Some jobs are better than others, but no job will make you happy if you are unhappy. If you are consistently dissatisfied, think about making changes within yourself before you look to change jobs again. You can find work you love but only when you're ready to.

TIP # 40
Everything takes time.

If you're in a hurry to get where you're going in life, slow down; you don't need to move so fast. As a recent graduate, you've been in school for some time and maybe you need to take a little time off. If you know what you want to do with your life, that's great—go for it! But if you're feeling overwhelmed by your many options and aren't sure of your direction, don't give in to the pressure to make a decision too quickly.

When surveyed about what they would have done differently after graduation if they knew then what they know now, a number of respondents interviewed for this book replied that they would have slowed down. Graduates face a lot of pressure to get a job and settle down but receive little encouragement to take time off or take their time making important life decisions.

Too many people rush through life. They complete one goal and quickly start working toward another. Are you in a hurry to get a job, get married, and start a family? Is that what you really want to do, or is that what you think you *should* be doing? If you're not sure, you're not ready to make a decision. Take time to reflect and relax. Let all you've learned sink in.

It may take years to become the person you want to be, so don't ignore the person you are today. Give yourself time to figure out what kind of work you want to do. Think about the city, state, or country in which you'd most like to live. Do you need to travel and visit other places before you decide?

Have you thought about the type of person you want to marry or the kind of marriage you want to have? Do you want to have children? Are you ready to be a good parent? Don't rush to take on more responsibility than you are ready to handle. Time is on your side. There's a difference between slacking and taking a little time off. Don't make excuses to avoid responsibility, but keep in mind that sometimes the most responsible choice is to wait to make a commitment to a job or a person. Never take on responsibility or obligations unless you're genuinely committed to meeting them.

Remember that patience is a virtue. It will take time for you to find an ideal job, and it will take time for you to earn and save the amount of money you want. You have to merit each promotion and pay increase you get.

In school, you and most of your classmates moved along at a similar pace, but in life, you move along at the pace you choose. Don't compare yourself to others; set your own pace.

Everything takes time, persistence, a game plan, belief in one-self, and the right attitude. Everyone starts somewhere. Even rich and famous people like actor Jim Carrey, software billionaire Bill Gates, and television icon Oprah Winfrey can tell a story of a time when things were different for them. Everyone must overcome struggles, challenges, and obstacles. Very few people start out at the top, but the tough times in life will help prepare you for the better times yet to come. Although it may be difficult to under-stand now, you will enjoy and appreciate what you have much more if you plan for it and work for it.

TIP # 41
Be yourself; you are enough.

On a plane ride home from Atlanta, I was thinking about all the work I had left to do before I could get my business up and run-ning. After spending several days with Susan Bixler, a successful and respected image consultant in Atlanta, I had earned my certi-fication as a corporate image consultant. Susan had written sev-eral books and established herself as an expert, and I wondered if I would forever be in her shadow. I wanted to establish my own credentials, not be the clone of someone else, yet I wasn't sure I was qualified to do it by myself.

I met with Gail, a friend of mine who is a psychologist, a few weeks later. I told her about some of my concerns and asked her to work with me on a few projects. I valued her insight and knew her credentials would be an asset.

Gail was flattered by my offer but declined the invitation to work with me. She leaned in closer and told me something I already knew but refused to believe. "You've got everything you need to succeed. You don't need me or my credentials." She knew I wasn't convinced and continued, "People might have awards and degrees decorating their walls, but many of them *hide* behind their credentials. They need to hear what you have to say. You don't need me or anyone else to help you—*you are enough.*"

Gail was right; she gave me some of the most valuable advice I've ever received. I began taking more risks and doing things *my* way. I reminded myself to be myself. I kept hearing Gail's words in my mind: *You are enough.*

It took time for me to find my own voice and establish myself as an expert. But only when I was true to myself, not trying to imitate someone else, did I really begin to excel.

Whether you believe it now or not, you really do have all you need to succeed. Be yourself. *You* are unique. You might have the same skills or interests as others, but only you do things the way *you* do. Be who you are; you can stand out and still fit in. People will respect you for being you. No matter how many people have come before you, there is no other you. Be yourself; *you are enough.*

TIP # 42
Pay attention to the proven practices of successful people.

Every tip in this book is written to help you succeed. You can read this or any other book written on achieving success, and although each successful individual has his or her own personal story to tell, there are some things almost all successful people have in common.

It's important to set goals and determine what you want, but knowing what you want is not enough to achieve it. Success doesn't just *happen*. You must be committed and motivated to succeed, work hard, develop good work habits, and maintain a winning attitude.

Most successful people have been where you are today. You don't have to learn everything on your own. Pay attention to the proven practices of successful people and increase your chances of success.

There are always exceptions, but generally you will find most successful people are:

1. Committed. Successful people believe in their vision, themselves, and others. If they say they will do something, they do it, and they do whatever it takes to get a job done well and on time.

2. Driven. Successful people are driven to succeed. They are purpose driven and driven in setting goals and then achieving them. They focus on their priorities, and they are fearless, relentless, and willing to take risks. Driven to do well, they often exceed expectations.

3. Team players. Successful people understand the value of collaborative efforts. Emphasizing we more than me, they bring people together and are able to appreciate and acknowledge each person's contribution.

4. Innovative. Successful people are creative thinkers and doers. They are not threatened by new ways of doing things; they think out of the box, generate new ideas, and are solution oriented.

5. Optimistic. Successful people are positive. They think positively, see potential, and focus on possibilities. They look for and see the good in other people, are "up" more than "down," and rebound quickly from a setback or problem.

6. Diligent workers. Successful people work hard, but because they enjoy what they do, it hardly seems like work. They don't watch the clock and anticipate the time to stop. They have specific tasks they want to complete, and only when they finish what they set out to do will they stop.

7. Passionate. Successful people are passionate about their work. Their personal resolve and enthusiasm are contagious and intriguing.

8. Courageous. Successful people are willing to confront problems and mend misunderstandings. They are willing to take a stand and when necessary are willing to stand alone. They give and accept honest feedback and always strive to improve. They are not afraid of failing or making a mistake and seek to learn something new when they do either.

Acquiring good work habits can increase your chances of success and help you maximize your natural talents and abilities. Identify and focus on the areas you should work on improving.

You don't have to learn the hard way or all on your own. Take your cue from those who are already where you want to be. *Pay attention to the proven practices of successful people.*

TIP # 43
Act confidently—even when you're not.

Robin, the personnel director of a large retail organization, knows she must be ready psychologically, emotionally, and physically to give her best performance every day. It helps her to think of the workplace as a big theatre. Her customers and coworkers carefully watch every move she makes, and she takes her performance at work just as seriously as she would if she were performing on stage. If she feels awkward or uncomfortable, others pick up on it and feel the same way. For others to have confidence in her, she must have confidence in herself. The more experience and knowledge she has, the more confident she is.

Confidence is built over time. It's not easy to feel confident when you don't know what you're doing, but no one expects you to know everything. If you are asked a question and you don't have the answer, admit you don't know. Don't belittle yourself for not knowing; always speak highly of yourself and focus on the things you do well.

Until you are as confident as you'd like to be, practice acting confidently. Stand a little taller and hold your head a little higher. Smile when you say hello. Give a nod and acknowledge the people you see. Shake hands firmly, speak assuredly and assertively, and always look directly at the person you are talking to.

Do more than put on an act; become the confident person you portray to others. Tap into the positive feelings you have when you really are confident as a result of doing something well.

Janie, an avid runner, is confident and secure when she runs but is uncomfortable in most social situations. As she worked on building her confidence when socializing, it helped her to tap into the power she feels when she runs. Try it yourself. The next time you need to boost your confidence, envision yourself doing something that makes you feel sure of yourself; then carry that feeling with you.

When you appear confident, others assume you are confident. No one knows when you're acting; people believe what they see. If you always act confidently, before you know it, you won't need to put on an act. One day you'll realize you've become the confident person you pretended to be. When you do, your overall performance will improve and you'll be performing at your best!

TIP # 44
Be a successful student of your own failure.

Most people seeking success do everything they can to avoid failure. We expect to succeed; we revere the most successful people and pity those who fail. Failure is viewed negatively, and we *fear* it. We're embarrassed when we fail. We often hide our failures and keep them to ourselves.

Yet most people fail before they succeed. Think about some of the successful people you know. How did they get where they are today? Have they always been successful?

Abraham Lincoln failed many times in his career but went on to succeed. He was defeated in elections and rejected for political office numerous times, but it didn't stop him from running again and becoming one of America's most recognized and respected presidents.

Thomas Edison failed thousands of times before he successfully invented the light bulb. He succeeded because he kept trying and never gave up.

Louisa May Alcott was told by an editor that she'd never write anything people would want to read, but that didn't stop her from writing. She went on to write the legendary *Little Women* and a number of other works.

Sylvester Stallone experienced his share of rejection and failure. His script for the movie *Rocky* was rejected more than

30 times before it was accepted, produced, and became a smash hit.

Michael Jordan was cut from his high school basketball team, but that didn't stop him. He kept on playing and trying and succeeded at his game, becoming the National Basketball Association's most famous player.

Barbra Streisand faced rejection; she was frequently told she wasn't pretty enough to succeed, but she didn't give up. She's a successful singer, actress, songwriter, and movie director.

Stephen Spielberg dropped out of college. Now he's a blockbuster movie producer and director using his platform to both entertain and educate his audiences.

J.K. Rowling, creator of Harry Potter, was broke and unemployed when she wrote her first manuscript. Once a struggling single mother, she's now one of Britain's wealthiest women.

Walt Disney suffered financial problems and a nervous breakdown before achieving fame and fortune and founding an animation and entertainment empire famous throughout the world.

People can fail many times and still succeed but only if they refuse to accept defeat. Successful people view failure as a temporary setback rather than a permanent resolution. They persevere, refuse to give up, and try over and over again. Don't be afraid of failing; anticipate failure—it's an important part of success. The more you look, the more you will see the benefits of failure.

Anticipate failure. Do what you can to avoid taking a big stumble or making mistakes, but don't be surprised when you do. Anticipate failure before success, knowing that most people fail many times before they succeed. When you acknowledge that you might fail, it will be less upsetting if you do.

Study and learn from failure. Be a student of your own failure; learn from your mistakes. Take the time you need to evaluate your failures. Determine what went wrong and why. Decide what needs to change and what you will do differently the next time around.

Let go of failure. Don't dwell on your failures. Instead, focus on your successes. Take the time you need to regroup, but don't wait too long to pick yourself up and start over again. Each time you fail, you're one step closer to success.

Give yourself credit for trying. Don't be ashamed of failing. Don't be too hard on yourself or think you're a fool; you didn't do anything so wrong. You've got nothing to be embarrassed about. People fail all the time. Those who never fail are those who never *try*. You're already ahead of others because you are willing to try.

Try again. Don't let your errors stop you from trying. If you want to move forward, you have to try over and over again. The more you try, the closer you will get to reaching a victory.

TIP # 45
Get rid of the chewing gum.

There's nothing professional about chewing gum. Like smoking, biting your nails, or continuously clearing your throat, it's a bad habit you're better off without. Chewing gum is unappealing whether you are sitting in a meeting, talking with someone in person, or talking on the phone. Even when you sit quietly working at your desk, your coworkers can hear your chewing.

Think about the things you do and the effects they have on others; be aware of your idiosyncrasies. Everyone has imperfections, but there's no need to draw attention to yours.

Heed the following:

- Get rid of the gum; don't chomp, smack, or make noises when you chew gum, suck on candy, or eat. Be aware of others when you are eating. Once while in a surgery waiting room (where patients had been without food or drink since midnight), I watched a woman at the nurse's desk chewing gum and snapping it loudly. Not only was it rude; it was thoughtless toward the surgery patients. Most were hungry and thirsty, since they had not had anything to eat or drink for a dozen hours or more. Even worse, other employees came and went with coffee and snacks even though they could have eaten in the cafeteria next door.

- Keep your hands folded in front of you when you don't know what else to do. Keep them out of your pants and pant pockets, out of your hair, and away from your face.

- Avoid nervous fidgeting; don't play with your rings, earrings, glasses, paper, or pen.

- Be still. Don't tap your fingers, pen, or pencil on the desk.

- Never pick your nose, your ears, your eyes, or teeth. If you need to remove something, go to the restroom to do it.

- Blow your nose in private when you can. If you must blow it in public, do so as quietly and discreetly as possible. Handle your tissue with care; no one should have to see what you've blown into it.

- Cover your mouth and turn away from others when you sneeze or cough.

- Don't file, clip, bite, or pick your fingers or toenails in public.

You need to know how to conduct yourself in a variety of situations. Whether you're at work or socializing with friends, make an effort to be your best. You will earn more respect when you act dignified and refined. People notice everything you do; make sure *you* pay attention too.

TIP # 46
Dress for the position you want.

The moment you begin your job search, you must present yourself as the person you plan to be. You may be used to wearing what you want each day, like your favorite jeans and T-shirts, but if you want to be taken seriously, you'd better give serious consideration to what you wear.

When you dress for work, what *you* want to wear isn't nearly as important as what your *employer* wants you to wear. If two people applying for a job have similar credentials but one of them *appears* more qualified, that person has an advantage in getting the job. When all else is equal, the person who *looks* most professional and successful almost always wins.

When you decide what to wear to an interview, don't choose clothing based on who you are *today*; choose clothing that reflects the person you are about to become. Dress as if you already have the job, and you will appear ready to tackle the position and responsibility of the job you are applying for

There are many talented, intelligent, and capable people who create barriers for themselves; don't let your clothing be a barrier. Poor hygiene and inappropriate dress hurts your image. If it appears that you can't handle the basics of personal grooming, why should a potential employer think you can carry out the duties of the job?

If you want to be noticed for your contributions, don't draw negative attention to yourself. If you are ready to take on more responsibility and want to be considered for a promotion, make it easy for others to *see* how ready you are and look like the responsible person you claim you are.

I've heard from numerous individuals who attribute a promotion to their dressing better than they needed to. I've also heard from managers who didn't promote someone because that person didn't look ready to take on more responsibility. When you look as though you are ready for advancement, others assume you are ready.

Emulate the people who are where you want to be. If the managers in your company wear suits, start wearing a suit. That action alone will change the perception others have of you. The more closely you resemble management, the easier it is for others to see that you are ready to move into a managerial position. Even if you were unsuccessful when you tried to draw attention to yourself before, the change in your appearance could make the difference.

Don't dress for the position you have. Dress for the position you want.

TIP # 47
Get involved.

Life is what you make it. You can choose to get involved in life or sit back and wait and see how your life unfolds. You can choose to be a doer or a talker, a giver or receiver, a leader or follower. You can sit back and do nothing or get involved and ensure you accomplish something. Experience life and continue to learn and grow. The best way to learn is by *doing*. Get involved in your life.

Get involved in your work. Do more than show up for work each day. Take on a new challenge, look for new and better ways of doing things, and volunteer to work on a project. The more you contribute, the more value you bring to your organization. The more involved you are, the more you will get out of the work you do.

Get involved with people. Develop strong relationships and connections with others. Keep in touch with former teachers, managers, customers, coworkers, and friends. These are some of your best connections, and staying in touch helps you build a strong network. It's easy to lose touch with people over the years, but it's enriching and beneficial for you to work at staying connected.

Get involved with a mentor. Spend time with people you admire, people who have done what you want to do, or people willing to help you and teach you something new. If your company has a mentoring program, enter it. If not, ask for a referral to one or find a mentoring program on your own. You'll find many people willing to help you if only you ask them to. You can learn a lot from a mentor—and from becoming a mentor, too. Stay involved in mentoring; once you're established in your career, offer to mentor someone who can benefit from you.

Get involved in industry associations. Do more than just join an association; work on a committee, plan an event, or take on a position in the association leadership. Don't join just because you think it will be good for *you;* join because you can contribute something to others too.

Get involved with your family and friends. Know what's going on in the lives of your family and friends and become interested in the things they do. Spend time with people; initiate a get together, and have meaningful conversations. Celebrate birthdays, anniversaries, and other occasions.

Get involved in your community. Read the local paper so you know what's going on, get to know your neighbors, and attend community meetings. Cast your vote when there's an election, learn about your elected officials, and become a part of your community.

Get involved in a cause. If you care about it, feel strongly about it, like to talk about it, and are passionate about it, do something about it. Your involvement (or lack of it) makes a difference. Don't sit back waiting for someone else to take the lead; step up and step out and take the lead yourself.

TIP # 48
Work hard, play hard.

Some people live life on automatic pilot. They get up each day at the crack of dawn, go to work all day, come home with just a few hours to spare, and then go to bed. They wake up again the next day and start their routine over again.

Work consumes many people, but it doesn't have to consume you. It's important to learn to separate your work life from your personal life. You shouldn't bring your personal life to work or make a habit of bringing work issues home with you.

When you work *harder*, you're not necessarily working *smarter*. Success isn't a result of the amount of time you put in each day; it's what you do with your time when you're working that counts. Don't waste your time away. Work on doing the most important things each day.

Some people work on weekends to catch up, but be careful if you do this. Everyone needs time away from work. It's good when you enjoy your job but important to have balance in your life too.

Spend time with family. Go for a walk, see a movie, shop, or play games. Spend quality time doing whatever you want. Sit back, relax, and talk as long as you're doing it with the people who mean the most to you.

Find a hobby. It will be easier to break away from work and give your attention to something else when it's something you really like to do. Get curious about something and take some time to learn more about it. Strive to have a variety of interests. It will make you a more interesting and well-rounded person.

Join a league or club. Do you like to bowl, play basketball or cards, ride a bike, read, or ski? If you do, find other people who enjoy the same thing and join them. It's more fun to do these things with someone else and a good way for you to be held accountable when you know others are counting on you.

Hang out with your friends. Remember how much fun you've had just hanging out with your friends? Friends are good for you; stay in touch with your friends and hang out the way you used to. If you don't make your friends a priority and work at maintaining relationships with them, your friendships will slip away.

Throw a party. If you don't have a reason to throw a party, find or create one. Be the one to bring people together.

Don't take life too seriously. All work and no play is no good for anyone. Enjoy the fruits of your labor. Live life and enjoy life. Get into the habit of working hard *and* playing hard.

TIP # 49
Put people first.

You've been encouraged to work hard and to set and achieve your goals. You know it's important to be a good person too. But what does that mean to you exactly? When important decisions must be made, will you put people first? Will you favor *people* over politics, money, and success? Or will you step over people if doing so will help you advance socially or economically?

You can put people first and still succeed. You can have a family and have a career too. But you *won't* if you put work before family or if you value making money more than making friends. Relationships are important in every aspect of your life. What fun is it to win an award if you have no one to share your excitement? Is a celebration any fun if you're celebrating by yourself?

Everyone has something to offer, but you must be open to receiving what others have to give.

No matter how high you rise, you're never above anyone else. No amount of money you make or power you have will make you a better person. You have to work at being a better person. Don't let your success go to your head.

The best and most successful people rarely succeed alone. Watch any awards program and notice how often several people come forward to accept each award. Time and time again, those giving their acceptance speech exceed the time limit thanking and acknowledging others. Rarely is an award won through the efforts of one person alone.

It's been said a dying man never wishes for more time to work but wishes instead for more time to spend with the *people* he cares most about. *People* are what matters. Cherish your relationships.

Nothing is more rewarding than creating and sharing your success with other people. Surround yourself with supportive people, and you will soar. Pay attention to the people in your life. You'll never regret putting people first.

Someday it will be your turn and *you* will be called upon to accept an award. What do you see—lots of people with you or you standing alone? I hope you have people around you and you exceed the time limit while thanking them, too.

Social Skills

Maintain Good Relationships and Work Cooperatively with Others

TIP # 50
Take responsibility for yourself and your relationships.

I write a workplace advice column. As a result, I've learned a lot about people. Over the years, I've noticed a common theme among the many questions I receive.

People usually write to me because of a problem, and the problem usually is *somebody else*.

The troubles I hear about tend to center on the horrid boss, the irritating coworker, or the annoying customer. Every question I receive is different, yet the core issues and concerns are remarkably similar. I've been writing my column for more than ten years, and I can recall only *one* letter I received in which the writer said, "I am the problem."

Don't get me wrong; there are bad bosses, bothersome coworkers, and unfair practices. I realize that the wrong people get promoted and the right people are let go. I know all isn't fair, bad things happen, and at times there's no bright side to look on. My job, however, is to give advice, and I try to provide some consolation.

I've noticed, too, that there is a common theme in the advice I give. Although each situation is unique, and I try to personalize my response, my overall message can be summed up in just a few words: *Take responsibility for your relationships.*

This isn't what most people expect or want to hear. Occasionally, I hear from a dissatisfied reader whose only reason for contacting me a second time is to tell me *I* am the problem!

If you struggle in your relationships or encounter problems with the majority of the people in your life, consider this: *Other people* might not be the problem; the problem might be the person looking back at you in the mirror.

It's much easier to focus on other people than it is to focus on ourselves, because we see them differently (and sometimes more clearly) than we see ourselves. We complain, we withdraw, we pout, we nag, and we lose sleep over other people, instead of taking a good look at ourselves. You may be powerless to change someone else, but you're the only one who has the power to change yourself.

Yes, there are difficult people; it's a fact of life. We don't get to choose our family members. The decisions we make about where we live and where we work give us some say in who our neighbors, bosses, or team members will be, but few people are able to hand pick the people they want to work with or live by.

Strong, healthy relationships require time, effort, and a *desire* to keep the relationship strong. Some relationships can't be resolved. Sometimes the best decision is also the most difficult.

I once heard a saying that has stuck with me over the years, and I try to live by the simplicity of the message. It summarizes the theme of my advice: "If it's to be, it's up to me."

Now it's up to *you: Take responsibility for yourself and your relationships.*

TIP # 51
Network, network, network.

When Lisa called to ask me to go with her to a party on Friday night, I said no. I'd had an exhausting week. I'd been working, studying, and trying to decide what to do about a shaky relationship I was trying to break off. I wanted to stay in my dorm room the entire weekend—*alone*.

"Come on," she pleaded. "Let's go check it out—we'll leave after ten minutes if it's not any good. You *need* to get out and meet other people." Lisa was insistent, and I didn't have the energy to resist. I was sure I wouldn't meet anyone worthwhile or have a good time, but I let her talk me into going anyway.

Over 25 years have passed since that night, yet every time I see or talk to Lisa, she reminds me to *thank her* for *forcing* me to go to the party that night—and I *always* do. You see, the party she *made* me go to was where I first met my husband, Steve.

College dorm parties probably aren't the first thing you think of when thinking about networking. As I look back and reflect, however, I can see the events of that night were networking *working* at its best.

Networking doesn't have to be difficult and complex; it shouldn't be work at all. It doesn't always take work to expand your network. It can come from the things you *do*.

Do you: Talk to and keep in touch with your family, coworkers, customers, and friends?

Do you: Converse with your neighbors or teachers, store clerks, security guards, or drivers?

Do you: Maintain relationships with friends, former teachers, advisors, or bosses?

Do you: Attend weddings, celebrations, parties, or informal gatherings?

Do you: Start conversations with the people you meet while waiting in line or sitting on a plane?

Do you: Affiliate with a church or synagogue, belong to any clubs or organizations?

Do you: Volunteer, devote time to a cause, or help others out in any way?

Do you: Spend time on the Internet, instant message, or use message boards?

If you *do* any of the preceding, you *do* have a network of people. You're networking (or *doing* it) without even knowing. When you network to give and to grow, you gain.

Network to give: Develop meaningful relationships; it's not the *number* of people you have accumulated in your address book that matters—it's the *number of people who matter* to you in your life.

The more genuine your relationships are, the better your network will be. Don't be consumed with what you *get* from your relationships; focus on what you can *give*. You'll find that the more you give, the more you eventually get. Stay in touch with people by phone, card, or e-mail or by meeting when you can for lunch. Give your time instead of your money. Give ideas or information instead of gifts.

Network to grow: Join a group, take a class, become part of a book, cooking, or other club. Join your alumni association, find a mentor, or take up a hobby or sport. Consider becoming a member of the Rotary or Chamber of Commerce or volunteering at your favorite charity. Get away from your desk and take a break with coworkers. Invite a client (or your boss) to lunch. Grow each time you meet someone new. Grow by learning something new about the people you already know; learn from the experiences and opinions of others. Grow by learning, grow by doing.

Network to gain: Expand your knowledge, widen your interests, and reach out to others. Learn by asking, learn by listening, and by *doing* whatever you can to build strong relationships. Gain from giving and growing your network, and see your network *working* for you.

Network to *give*, Network to *grow*, Network to *gain*.
Network, Network, Network.

TIP # 52

Show up for events; your presence matters.

Melissa always felt uncomfortable when someone she knew experienced the loss of an important person. "I didn't know what to say or do," she told me. So, like many of us, she hesitated to call and stayed away, not because she didn't care but because she cared so much she didn't want to do or say the wrong thing. Instead, she rationalized, "They won't notice if I'm there or not."

Melissa's feelings are common. It's ironic that at times when people need us most, we hold back. Instead of attending to someone else's problem, we end up nurturing our *own*. Sometimes we *think* we know how someone feels, but we *don't*. That's why so many people turn to support groups for comfort. Whether it's an addiction, a trauma, or a loss, no one understands better than those who have been there.

Showing your support isn't limited to people who are suffering; it's important to be there in times of need *and* celebration. You'll be invited to many events over the years. Make an effort to attend. Whether it's a wedding, baby shower, retirement party, or birthday, celebrate the special occasions in life.

It's never too late to acknowledge someone. By the time I heard about Kay's loss, it was *after* her father's funeral. Since I couldn't attend the funeral, I called to express my condolences and planned on sending a card. I didn't get around to sending the card for several months and hesitated before I did, wondering if too much time had passed.

Kay was so touched by my card she called to *thank me* for sending it, saying it came at the *perfect* time. The card I sent arrived on the three-month anniversary of her father's death—a day she was feeling especially sad and alone. She said the onslaught of cards and calls immediately following his death was a bit overwhelming, but receiving them helped her get through each day. By the time my card arrived, the others had stopped coming. Receiving my card reminded her people still cared.

It's never too late (and *always* appreciated) to tell someone you care. Let people know you're thinking about them. Send a note or card, make a call, or, better yet, bring in a meal.

Sadly, Melissa learned about dealing with loss the hard way. "It does matter if you attend," she said. "I can tell you who among my friends was at the wake and funeral. Friends of mine who never met my dad came to the wake. It didn't matter if they stayed five or fifty minutes. It's a show of support and respect. *It matters.*"

She also learned how easy it is for people to say, "Let me know if I can do anything" but how hard it is to follow through. She said it helps to hear people say, "I'm here for you no matter what happens."

Be there for people; your presence matters.

TIP # 53
Just say "NO."

You might be used to hearing it but feel uncomfortable saying it.

You know it isn't hard to say but struggle with it every day.

You can hear "no" in your head, so why does "yes" come out instead?

You want to help others and make them feel good, but sometimes when you do, *you* end up feeling *bad*. Perhaps it's because whenever you say "yes" to something, you say "no" to another. It is impossible to do everything you want; time is too limited and life too busy. When you accept more to do than your time allows, you create needless stress for yourself. It's much better, although not always easier, to say "no" up front when you need to.

Saying no isn't easy. Adults of *all* ages struggle with saying it every day. "No" can sound harsh and negative. Even so, there are times *no* other response will do.

So what will you do if your manager asks you to dinner and you feel uncomfortable going? What will you say if the client you're with inappropriately touches your leg? Will you say *something* or *nothing* at all? Saying "no" in such situations is crucial, because it lets people know that they have crossed your boundaries.

What will you do when you're asked to head a committee, take on extra work, or help out a friend? What if you want to say "no" but aren't really sure?

When you're not sure how to answer:

1. **Consider your options.** Some requests are critical; they need to be done right away. Some people have authority; when your boss tells you to do something, you might have no choice at all. Know the difference between a command and an option. If you're ever unsure, *ask*.

2. **Get the facts.** Find out more about the request to make the right decision. "When do you need this by?" "Tell me what this is about." "How much time does it involve?"

3. **Take time to think.** Don't let people pressure you to say something you'll regret. Request some time to make your decision. "I need some time before I make a decision." "I need to look at my schedule." "I'll get back to you tomorrow."

4. **Make a decision.** Say "yes" when it is something you decide to do and "no" to everything else.

5. **Stand by your decision.** When you've taken the steps to make a well-thought-out decision, stick with it. You may disappoint someone, but it's better than disappointing yourself.

6. **Announce your decision.** If your answer is no, say "no." Don't *try* saying it, and don't make excuses for saying it. Say it any way you want:

No. No, thank you. No, I can't. No, I won't. Not now. No, I'm not interested. No, I'm not. No, you're not. No, we shouldn't. I won't be able to do it. Not a chance. I'd like to help you out, but I have to say no. I've decided not to do it. I decided against it. It's not going to happen. It won't work out for me. I'm saying no. No, I'm declining. No, I'm already committed. Thank you for asking, but no. No, it's not going to work out. I'm sorry to say this, but the answer is *no*.

Don't make it fancy or complicated. Speak up and simply say "*NO!*"

TIP # 54
Rate your shake.

If you were asked to define, and then teach, the art of giving a "perfect" handshake, what words would you use to describe it, and how would you teach others to shake hands? Do you think a handshake should be hearty, forceful, mild, or meek? What temperature and texture is best? Does it matter if hands are warm or cold, the texture rough or smooth? How firm a grip should there be? How tight a squeeze? How long should it last and how many "shakes" up and down? Does one size fit all or should a shake vary, depending on gender or the size of the hand?

If you never thought about it before, it's obvious there is more to a great shake than extending your hand. A *good* shake bonds people together; a *bad* shake leads to mistrust. A strong and enthusiastic shake says "I respect you." A half-hearted shake says "I don't care."

Shaking hands is the *only* "safe" touch there is. In business it is expected; in other circumstances, it is appreciated. A handshake adds friendliness to your greeting and reveals how you feel about yourself and others.

Rate your shake. Circle the words best describing your shake.

Texture: Dry, sticky, clammy, rough, smooth, callused, soft

Temperature: Hot, warm, cool, cold

Grasp: Complete, partial, incomplete

Grip: Strong, solid, moderate, tame, shaky

Touch: Rigid, steady, flexible, relaxed, fragile

Squeeze: Tight, firm, mild, gentle

Duration: Lengthy, brief, rushed, abrupt

Feel: Spirited, selfish, assuring, considerate, questioning, anxious

An effective handshake connects two people, but there are other influencing factors. If your *body* sends a different message from the one you send through your *hand,* you create confusion.

Lack of eye contact, no expression, poor posture, or a questioning tone of voice weakens even the best shake. When your shake flows with the way you *look, act,* and *sound,* your rhythm and message flow too.

When your hands are dry and warm, and you have a solid and complete grip of the other person's hand, you are saying, "I'm confident and ready to meet you." When your touch is steady and your squeeze is firm, the message is "I'm focused and I genuinely care about you." And when the duration is brief and the "feel" assuring, you're saying, "I know what I'm doing. Don't worry about a thing."

Ten steps to a great shake.

1. Smile.
2. Make eye contact.
3. Nod.
4. Extend arm.
5. Step forward.
6. Grasp hand.
7. Grip solidly.
8. Squeeze firmly.
9. Pump twice.
10. Let go.

The right shake is a result of focus and practice; practice shaking hands with someone you trust. *Shake,* then *rate* your shake, until you're comfortable you've got it right.

TIP # 55
The company party is not a party.

If your idea of a good party includes heavy drinking, cozy (and cuddly) conversation, dirty dancing, or winning the title of *worst* karaoke singer, you're probably not going to think the company party is a party at all. I'm not suggesting you won't, or can't, have a good time; I'm merely suggesting you tone it down a bit.

Whether it's the company picnic, the holiday party, a convention, or someone's retirement or promotion during happy hour, social events can provide you opportunities to strengthen your relationships with coworkers. Act as if your behavior is being observed every minute, because *it is.*

If you wonder if your attendance matters, it does. You might not be *required* to attend, but your absence will be noted. When you are a "no show," you *show* you are not interested. This does not help you look like a committed team player or caring coworker.

If you can't decide what to wear, think *business event*, not *social event.* You are a professional; *look like one.* If it isn't a company picnic, don't even consider wearing jeans, tank tops, or shorts. If it isn't a costume party, don't wear anything so shocking or unusual that your clothing is the topic of conversation. If it isn't a black-tie formal affair, don't wear full-length, slinky, or sequined dresses or a tuxedo. And if it isn't a swimming party (which most business events are not), *never* bare your midriff, your buttocks, or breasts.

If you're planning on arriving fashionably late, make another plan. Late is late. There is nothing fashionable about it.

If alcohol is served, *think* **before you drink.** If you get wasted, you've *wasted* a valuable opportunity to demonstrate your self-control. You don't have to apologize or make excuses for not drinking, but when you drink and get drunk, you do. A small amount of alcohol is all it takes to affect your behavior.

If you want to stand out and be noticed, get up and move around. You are at a social event; *socialize.* Don't huddle in a bunch with your work buddies; get up and move around. People can't see you, let alone notice you, when you're sitting in the corner.

If you see people you do not know, introduce yourself. This is an ideal time for you to introduce yourself to those you don't ordinarily see or get to talk to, including company executives. But don't brown-nose, brag about your accomplishments, or ask for a raise or promotion; it is the *least-ideal* time to accomplish that.

If you're hoping to work out problems or discuss the latest gossip, keep hoping. You're at a party, and conversation should be festive, so keep it light and upbeat. People look forward to celebrations. You don't want to be a downer and spoil the celebratory mood. Make sure *you're* not the topic of conversation back at work when the party's over!

If you don't know if you should bring a casual date, don't. Just because you're invited to bring a guest doesn't mean you have to. You're responsible for your date, and you might feel more relaxed without someone by your side. If your date gets drunk or acts inappropriately, it will be a negative reflection of *you.*

If you feel uninhibited, control yourself. I don't care how long you've wanted to tell your cube mate you think she (or he) is "hot"; this is *not* the appropriate time. Nor should you take over the dance floor or kiss your boss (or someone else's spouse) under the mistletoe. No kissing, no hugging, and no "hanging on" to people. Remember where you are. The party is an extension of your workplace.

If you want to leave and you don't see the people you'd like to thank, don't leave. Your host and hostess will remember who said hello and good-bye. Always do both, and never leave without saying thank you. It's the appropriate and most gracious thing to do.

TIP # 56

Always have your business card with you.

It was a beautiful sunny day in Ixtapa, Mexico, and my husband and I were relaxing on the beach. The couple next to us asked where we were from, and within a few minutes we were bantering back and forth.

David was intrigued when I told him about my business. "I am on the board of a company that could use your services," David told me. "I've got a meeting with them when I get back. I need to get your business card before we leave tomorrow."

My husband looked at me and said, "This sounds exciting. You've got your business cards with you, right?" I was *hoping* I did but wasn't really sure. After all, I was *supposed* to be on vacation. I was trying not to think too much about business.

Back in the room, I searched for my business cards. "Don't *you* have one of my cards?" I asked my husband. He didn't say a word, but I knew what he was thinking: *How can you have your own business, coach people toward success, and not carry business cards with you?*

I looked through my purse, my suitcase, and everywhere else, but I couldn't find even one business card.

David understood when I told him I must have given my last card away, which was easier for me to say than admitting I didn't bring any. So he exchanged cards with *my husband* instead, my name and number hand-written on the back.

David and I connect through e-mail every now and then, but I haven't done any work for him yet. He never did have *my* business card for the meeting. I'll never know if it made a difference to him, but I do know it made a difference to *me.*

I decided that no matter *where* I am, I will always be prepared and *always have my business cards with me!*

*Save yourself embarrassment; be prepared, and **always** have your business cards (or resume) with you!*

TIP # 57

Never go to a business event hungry.

If you are the type of person who doesn't eat when you have an event later in the day in order to save your appetite, you might want to change your ways.

If you attend an event and you are thinking about how hungry you are, you're thinking about the wrong thing. Whether you are at a conference, a trade show, a banquet, or meeting someone in a restaurant, focus on the reason you are there. It isn't just to eat.

You should never to go to a business event hungry because:

- If you're focused on the food, you're not focused on the people.
- Drinking alcohol on an empty stomach is likely to have a stronger effect on you.
- If you're watching the time and looking for food, you're wasting the time you should be talking with others.
- You're likely to eat too fast and too much, which is not a good combination for your stomach or your manners.
- You're likely to start eating before you should, and you should always wait for others to be seated and served before you begin to eat.
- You'll be so busy eating that you might forget to pass the bread or the butter or the dressing.
- You won't want to stop eating to start talking, so you'll either miss out on conversation or end up talking with food in your mouth.
- If you get something stuck in your tooth, your fear that someone will clear your plate might prevent you from leaving the table to get it out.

- If you rush to eat, you won't have the advantage of waiting and watching what others are doing, and you'll increase your chances of making a mistake.

When you are hired to work in a professional position, you are expected to behave in a professional manner at *all* times. If you behave unprofessionally, you are not fulfilling your obligations. Never rush to order, eat large amounts of food, or eat too quickly. Make the most of every opportunity you have, or you may not get the chance to prove yourself again.

TIP # 58
Stop talking.

"I dread my lunches with Jane," Leslie told me. "She delves into such detail; a five-minute story takes her 30 minutes to tell. She doesn't like e-mail, but when we talk on the phone, even if I tell her I only have a minute, she goes on and on and I can't get off of the phone."

Some people don't know when to stop talking. They think others want to hear every little detail, but they don't. Evan worked hard to increase sales in his territory. He found a solution to every problem, except one: his own. He never stopped talking. His coworkers said he suffered from diarrhea of the mouth. I can't think of a less-desirable image.

I was greeting people as they walked into the training room. Typically, I get a two-to-three sentence response when I ask people about themselves, but when I asked Ron what type of work he did, his response never ended: "I just started a new job, but I'm waiting to hear about another one. If I do, I'll end up moving. I moved here three years ago for a job, but one year later, the company was sold. My girlfriend gave up a good job to come here. She has a good job now, but it took her awhile to find it. She wants to go part time to spend more time with our son. We got married last year, went to Vegas for our honeymoon. We wanted to go back for our anniversary, but didn't have anyone to look after our son. It's tough with no family here, so we don't get out much, but the neighbor took him one night. We saw a movie. It was the night of that awful storm. The electricity went out, and I had frozen meat in the freezer I had to throw out. I bought it to save money, but ended up wasting it instead, which is how I feel every time I fill my car up with gas...."

Ron went on and on. He was having a conversation with himself. Whether you are looking for a job, meeting customers, networking, or socializing with friends, when people ask you about yourself, they are asking for the 30-second commercial, not for the unedited version of your entire life.

People want to participate in a conversation; stop talking long enough to listen to what others have to say. If you want to increase your chances of receiving a job offer, making a sale, or impressing someone on a first date, you need to know when it's time for you to stop talking.

I know you want (and need) to sell yourself to an employer, a prospect, or someone you want to impress, but be careful not to oversell yourself. When you stop talking, you pick up cues you'd otherwise miss. If you like to hear yourself speak, listen to yourself ask the right questions.

Here are some good questions to help make a conversation successful:

"What's the biggest challenge you face in your business?"

"What type of work do you do?"

"How did you get into that line of work?"

"What do you like best about what you do?"

"Tell me about yourself."

You don't have to talk a lot to become more interesting. Some of the most interesting, successful, and popular people don't say much at all. They know when to stop saying "I" and make a habit out of saying "you." They listen more than they talk, and when you stop talking, *you* will too.

TIP # 59

Be friendly, but don't be a flirt.

Ted and I were sipping coffee as we waited for the crew to change the set. We were producing a training video, and I was spending the week in his home town. When he inquired about the hotel I was staying at, I didn't think anything of it. When he proceeded to tell me why he wanted to know, however, I did think it was a bit strange.

"I almost checked into your hotel last night." Ted told me. I didn't ask him why, but he was determined to tell me more. "I didn't sleep very well last night. The couch in my family room isn't very comfortable for sleeping—I ended up sleeping on it last night because my wife kicked me out of our bed."

I didn't know what to say—Ted was a casual business acquaintance, and we hadn't talked much about our personal lives before. I had just met his wife the night before when we all had dinner together, and I felt uncomfortable with the way he was talking about her. Hearing the intimate details of their sleeping arrangement was something I didn't need or want to know about.

I wondered why Ted was telling me such personal information. Did he want me to feel sorry for him? Was he turning to me for comfort? What kind of response was he hoping for? Most important, would he have said the same thing to me if I were a *man*?

That night, as I was having dinner with Kathy, who was working on the project with us, she mentioned she thought Ted was interested in me. When I asked her why, she said she could tell by the way he acted around me. When I told her about my conversation with Ted earlier that day, she wasn't surprised—she was certain he was *flirting* with me.

It's not always easy to tell when someone is flirting with you. Flirting can be healthy and fun when done in the right place and at the right time. Flirting with someone you are attracted to is fine when you are at a party and in most social situations, but it is not something you should do at work or any work-related function.

You may think you are being playful when you tease someone or make a sarcastic remark, but your comment may be misunderstood. Play it safe and act appropriately at all times.

Most coworkers engage in casual conversation from time to time. It's natural to talk about vacations, family, and hobbies, but it can become awkward if you pry too deeply or offer too much information.

You will be meeting many new people over the years, and it is likely you will encounter people you are interested in getting to know on a more personal level. When you do, be discreet. Make arrangements to meet away from work to get to know each other.

Always be friendly, but when you are at work, *don't be a flirt*.

TIP # 60
Mind your manners.

Display good manners *with people.*

DO:	DON'T:
Listen attentively.	Interrupt someone.
Take an interest in others.	Ask personal questions.
Hold the door open for others.	Slam the door on someone.
Arrive on time.	Make someone wait for you.
Bite your lip.	Say it if it isn't nice.
Smile.	Wink, sneer, or snicker.
Look at the person you are with.	Eye someone up and down.
Remember names.	Assume a nickname is preferred.
Say "please" when making a request.	Make demands.
Show your appreciation.	Take advantage of people.

(continues)

(continued)

DO:	DON'T:
Turn off your cell phone.	Take a call when with others.
Say "thank you" when complimented.	Refuse or negate a compliment.
Drive defensively.	Gesture at or intimidate drivers.
Accept responsibility.	Cast blame on others.
Offer help.	Shun people in need.
RSVP promptly.	Forget to respond.
Send thank you notes.	Send e-mail instead.
Use good grammar.	Use slang or profanity.

Display good manners *at work.*

DO:	DON'T:
Keep your hands to yourself.	Touch (except to shake hands).
Greet coworkers each day.	Talk too much at work.
Introduce yourself.	Use first names unless requested.
Attend meetings.	Talk during a meeting.
Treat men and women equally.	Make sexual or sexist remarks.
Work efficiently; focus on your job.	Use work time for personal tasks.
Dress for work.	Dress haphazardly.
Get to know your coworkers.	Gossip about other people.
Wear name tags on right shoulder.	Refuse to wear a name tag.
Initiate conversation with others.	Monopolize a conversation.
Follow through on your promises.	Break commitments.
Visit with coworkers over lunch.	Ignore others or leave them out.
Pick up after yourself.	Expect others to do it for you.
Learn about cultural differences.	Ignore or judge differences.

Display good manners *when dining.*

DO:	DON'T:
Think before you drink.	Drink to get drunk.
Keep your hand available for greetings.	Become preoccupied with eating.
Put your napkin on your lap immediately.	Wipe your mouth—dab it instead.
Pass the salt and pepper together.	Pass one without the other.
Taste your food before seasoning.	Salt your food automatically.
Pass food counterclockwise.	Allow food to pile up by you.
Cut a few pieces at a time.	Pre-cut food and then dig in.
Spoon your soup *away* from you.	Blow on or slurp your soup.
Order something easy to eat.	Order messy finger foods.
Take your time as you dine.	Rush through the meal.
Chew your food thoroughly.	Talk with food in your mouth.
Position your silverware when done.	Push your plate away from you.
Excuse yourself when necessary.	Pick your teeth at the table.
Tip generously.	Eat out if you can't afford a tip.

You may have learned these rules before or think manners are old fashioned. The truth is that manners *never* go out of style. They are every bit as important today as they were years ago. When you display good manners, you show respect for others. Treat everyone you meet courteously, regardless of age, gender, race, or ethnicity. When you do, you look good. You will be valued as an employee, friend, and colleague. Whatever you do, always remember to mind your manners.

TIP # 61

Balance screen time with face time.

Have you ever wondered what life was like generations ago? How did people manage without all of the modern conveniences we've become accustomed to? Can you imagine your day-to-day life without a television to watch, a computer to log on to, or a phone to use for communication?

Sometimes I get tired of talking on the phone. I often wish I wasn't compelled to check my e-mail or turn on the TV and wonder if I do it out of habit. Sometimes I'm not sure if these things *simplify* my life or *complicate* it. Previous generations missed out on the technological advantages we have, and in some ways life was more difficult. In other ways, it might have been easier. They had fewer distractions and, as a result, more *face time,* which is something we are in short supply of.

Did you know that the average American child will spend more time in front of the television than in school? Do you have any idea how many adults spend more time interacting with a computer screen than interacting with people?

We've become a nation of "screen addicts." This is not a good thing; sitting in front of a computer or watching TV is *not* good for you. Research has found that TV watching leads to unhealthy eating habits and obesity. We eat too much of the wrong food and sit idle too much of the time.

Spending time in front of a screen doesn't help relationships or families either. Good communication is paramount to any relationship and can't compete with a television or computer.

Although e-mail often is used as a means of staying in touch with people, it is not equivalent to time spent with someone. It is easy to hide behind e-mail and escape the responsibilities of a real relationship.

If you are in a relationship with someone and spend most of your time in front of a screen, you are putting your relationship at risk. It is difficult to devote your attention to someone when you are paying attention to the screen. If your job involves time in front of a screen, remind yourself to look up every now and then. If you have something important to communicate, do it face to face. Communication is more effective that way.

Technology has enriched our lives; we have the ability to get news in an instant and connect with people anywhere and any-time. Use it to your advantage, but remember: *Technology is no substitute for human contact.*

The next time you pick up the phone to make or take a call, *stop* before you do.

Is the person you're about to talk to *more important* than whoever you are with? If so, complete the call. If not, put down the phone, face the person you are with, and have a conversation.

The next time you're about to log on to your computer, stop before you do.

Look at your watch; it's easy to lose track of time when you use the computer. If you decide to continue, give yourself a time limit. Ask yourself: Is my time better spent interacting with *some<u>one</u>* or interacting with *some<u>thing</u>*? A computer screen is a thing; you're probably better off spending time with a person.

The next time you reach for the remote, *stop* before you do.

Do you want to *watch* life or *live* life? People tend to watch TV to alleviate boredom or loneliness. Are you bored? Are you lonely? Are you avoiding something or someone? *Do you think you should be turning on the TV or turning to someone instead?*

The key is balance; balance screen time with face time.

TIP # 62
Look for similarities, not differences.

I greeted the driver as I got into the backseat of the cab. It was a snowy night, and my flight had been delayed, and all I could think about was getting to my hotel and going to bed.

The driver was friendly, welcomed me to his hometown, and asked me why I was there. Although I typically like to strike up conversations, I wasn't really in the mood that night, but the driver was relentless. He wanted to hear about the conference I was speaking at the next day and was genuinely interested in learning more about me.

I began to respond to his enthusiastic manner and asked him a few questions too. He told me about his escape from Cuba when he came to the United States, about the boat he made out of old truck tires, and how he lived in hiding prior to his daring escape. He described his dangerous departure during a heavy rainstorm, how he almost died en route, and how he was miraculously rescued.

I was captivated by his amazing story of survival. He had such a positive outlook, was filled with gratitude, and so proud to be an American citizen. I learned about his three daughters, who ironically were close in age to my own three girls, and discovered his challenges and concerns as a parent were no different from mine.

When I got into the cab that night, our differences were obvious. I assumed we came from different backgrounds, worked different types of jobs, and lived very different lives. Yet, in less than an hour, I realized we had more in common than I thought. We both loved our families and had similar hopes and dreams for our daughters. We both enjoyed talking to and learning about other people. And it was through our differences that I was able to understand, in a way I never had before, why and how people risk their lives to come to America. As a result of our conversation, I was reminded how grateful I am to be a citizen of the United States, which I admit I often take for granted.

When I arrived at the hotel and got out of the cab, I smiled at Felix, and he smiled at me. "Good luck with the girls," we said simultaneously. We laughed and then did it again: "It was great talking with you," we said in unison.

I thanked him for the ride and handed him my money. I picked up my suitcase, and then, as if on cue, we smiled and shook our heads, turned around, and said good-bye.

As a result of meeting Felix that night, *I am different* when I meet people who are different from me. I find myself looking for our *similarities* instead of focusing on our *differences*. And you know what? More often than not, I end up finding what I'm looking for.

TIP # 63
Bring out the best in others.

When Mike enters a room, people notice. When he speaks, people listen. He doesn't have to say much to command attention.

Ann's been referred to as a "people magnet." People surround her. If she won a contest, she'd earn the title "Miss Congeniality."

You probably know people who remind you of Mike or Ann. They are special because they do something special; they bring out the best in others. They both like people and people like them.

If people *like you*, they are more apt to buy from you, hire you, and promote you. People will trust you, confide in you, and help you, but only if they like you. Being likeable has many advantages; how likeable are *you?*

- **Do you like people?** Do you enjoy being around people? Are you the first to say hello or strike up a conversation? Or do you look away, pretending you don't see someone who is there? Are you interested in people and what they have to say?

- **Do you care about other people?** Do you ask people how they are doing and listen to their answers? When you meet someone, do you remember that person when you meet again? Are you able to remember names and the details of previous conversations? When you genuinely like and care about people, you should ask them questions and remember the answers you hear. When you care enough to remember, you show how much you care.

● **Do you make people smile?** When you see someone, do you see a smile? Or do people look away, avoiding contact? Notice the expressions of the people you see; it's likely a reflection of you. If you tend to see a lot of unhappy people, look at *yourself*. Smile often and share your smile with others. When you do, there's a good chance you'll see more smiles smiling back at you.

● **Do you like yourself?** The more comfortable you are with yourself, the more comfortable you will be with others. When you like and accept yourself, it's easier to like and care about other people.

● **Do you bring out the best in people?** What do you look for in people? Do you see good qualities or focus on the bad? Do you criticize, sit in judgment, or offer unsolicited advice? People are hard enough on themselves—they don't need anyone else to remind them of their imperfections. Look for the good in people.

Four steps to a more likeable you:

1. **Acknowledge the people you see.** Smile, make eye contact, and say hello.

2. **Show how much you care.** Be interested in others; ask questions, and then listen to the answers. Listen more than you talk.

3. **Remember people.** Remember and use names. Remember and follow up on prior conversations.

4. **Bring out the best in people**. Look for and point out the good in people through praise, words of encouragement, and sincere compliments.

When you make people feel important, you become important to them. When you make people look good, you look good too. Bring out the best in others; *when you bring out the best in others, you bring out the best in yourself.*

TIP # 64
Show your appreciation.

You are a unique individual. You have talents and abilities that differentiate you from everyone else. You are different, yet you are also more like other people than you may realize. Aside from common survival needs, people need to be acknowledged for the things they do and for who they are. Everyone craves appreciation.

People seek to satisfy this craving in different ways. Some people enjoy being in the spotlight; others are embarrassed by public praise. For some, it doesn't matter *how* they are acknowledged, as long as they are appreciated. How do you like to be acknowledged? Even if you are satisfied with yourself, it's still important to be reassured by someone else.

When you show your appreciation to others, you will get back some of what you give. Appreciation is *always* appreciated. You can earn the cooperation and dedication of your coworkers by showing your appreciation. This can be more than saying "thanks" or writing a thank you note. There are limitless ways to convey your appreciation. Here are just a few.

Seven ways to show your appreciation:

1. **Write a letter**. Go beyond a thank you note; write a letter expressing your sincere appreciation and how you've benefited from what the person did.

2. **Offer to run an errand.** If you're going out and will be near the post office, drycleaner, deli, or coffee shop, ask if you can drop off or pick up something for someone.

3. **Help someone.** Show your appreciation by helping someone. Offer to make copies of something if you're heading to the copier, or deliver a fax you found in the fax machine. You can offer your help, but you will make a bigger impression if you do something without being asked.

4. **Bring a treat.** Does a coworker or friend like chocolate chip cookies, popcorn, or lattes? Get something the person will enjoy and bring it to him or her as a way of showing your appreciation.

5. **Be a sounding board.** Ask how things are going, and listen to the response.

6. **Buy a gift.** Is your friend or coworker a cat lover? Get him or her a cat picture frame. Is he or she a golfer? Buy him or her a few new golf balls or other golf-related items. You don't have to spend a lot of money to show your appreciation. Never give something in the hopes someone will be indebted to you; give with no strings attached. And be careful whom you give to; some companies don't allow employees to accept or exchange gifts.

7. **Share information.** If you know that someone has a particular interest, bring in an article on the subject, give a subscription to a magazine or new journal, or talk about some information you heard.

When you acknowledge what people do, they will notice *you*. Showing your appreciation is a powerful motivator. When you value and appreciate people, you are fulfilling a basic human need. Get in the habit of noticing and appreciating what others do. They will benefit and so will you.

Self-Discipline

Be Healthy, Wealthy, and Wise

TIP # 65

Get in shape and stay in shape.

You know it's important to your health to be in good shape. You're aware of the benefits of fitness, and you know what to do. You try to make it a priority, but have you succeeded? Are you in good shape? Are you doing your part to make sure you stay in shape? Do you like what you see when you look in the mirror? Or have you stopped looking because you don't like what you see?

We talk about health and exercise, and we talk about losing weight. When it comes to getting in shape and staying in shape, there is a substantial amount of information on the subject, including the health risks of being overweight. Yet obesity continues to rise, and people become more sedentary every year.

You may look great, but are you as active as you were a few years ago? Are you gaining weight or staying the same? Once you've reached your final height, you should determine and maintain a final weight. Some people can eat all they want and remain thin because that's the way their metabolism functions, but most people's bodies do not work like that. No matter how thin you are or have been, you are likely to gain weight as you age.

You can avoid the gym and avoid the numbers on the scale, but you can't hide it when you are overweight and out of shape. Don't worry about looking or being *perfect*; focus on being healthy and living a healthy lifestyle. Don't just *get* in shape; *stay* in shape. You will feel better when you maintain a healthy shape and size. While some people stay in shape with little effort, most people have to work at it. As you consider your career and life goals, don't overlook *yourself*. Set realistic goals for your *health*.

The discipline it takes to stick with an exercise program will carry over into other areas of your life and benefit you in other numerous ways. For every excuse you can come up with not to exercise, there is a reason why you should.

Don't have enough time? Make time. Watch one less television show, make one less phone call, or get up 20 minutes earlier. If you can't find the time, look for it—it's there.

Don't enjoy it? Make it fun. Exercise with a friend. Listen to music or a book on tape while you exercise.

Can't get motivated? Reward yourself. Whether it's going out to dinner, to a movie, or watching your favorite show, reward yourself for exercising. Don't sabotage your efforts by rewarding yourself with a hot fudge sundae. If food is the reward that works for you, choose a healthier, less-fattening alternative. Better yet, reward yourself by doing something you enjoy but only if you follow through with your exercise.

Can't commit to a regimen? Include exercise in your daily routine. Stretch while you brush your teeth. Take the stairs instead of the elevator. Park farther away and walk to your destination.

Don't feel well? Exercise is good medicine. Move and you will feel better.

Don't want to? Get up and do some type of aerobic movement for ten minutes; then reevaluate. Chances are your mood will change and you'll want to keep moving, but if you don't, at least you'll feel better knowing you did something instead of nothing.

Overwhelmed? Start small. Any movement is better than no movement.

- **Embarrassed to exercise around other people?** Go for a walk or a bike ride, jump rope in your garage, climb the steps, or buy an exercise machine to use at home.

- **Lonely?** Find an exercise partner, take a class, or walk a dog. If you don't have a dog, volunteer to walk someone else's.

- **Bored?** Make it fun. Watch television while you exercise. Find new ways to challenge yourself. Look—really look—at scenery, houses, or what's in your exercise room.

- **Stressed-out?** Exercise is a great stress reliever.

- **Tired?** Exercise can increase your energy and stamina.

- **Down in the dumps?** Exercise improves your attitude, clarity, and thinking.

- **Hungry?** Exercise can help curb your appetite. Drinking water is good for you and will fill you up too. Drink water before, during, and after exercising; drink water all day long!

Exercise doesn't have to be hard work, you don't have to sweat or work-out for an hour at a time to benefit. Always check with your doctor before starting a new exercise program, and once you get the okay, find the exercise best suited for you. Don't put it off any longer. Start moving and start reaping the rewards *today*.

TIP # 66
Eat to live; don't live to eat.

Ten years ago I changed my attitude toward food. I was healthy in every other way, and I couldn't understand why I had little energy and frequent headaches. When a friend suggested I make an appointment with an acupuncturist and natural healer, I was skeptical, but I had nothing to lose but my headaches. I wasn't getting the results I wanted from traditional medicine, and I was willing to try *anything* to feel better.

The healer suggested a number of homeopathic remedies and supplements, but for it all to work, I had to change my attitude toward food. Food sensitivities can cause all sorts of ailments. He gave me a strict diet to follow. It was difficult to stick to it, but my desire to *feel good* was stronger than my craving for any food or drink.

Within days I felt better. After a few weeks I had more energy. Over time, other people noticed the difference in me. I lost some weight, my skin was clearer, and I looked healthier (and some people said younger) than before. I was more in tune with myself and in control. Even my attitude changed for the better.

I've always been health-conscious, and I thought I was eating healthy foods. As I paid more attention to food labels, however, I discovered I was ingesting all sorts of ingredients I couldn't even pronounce.

You, too, might think you are making healthy choices. Choosing a can of juice over a soda may seem better for you, but many juices have just as much or more sugar than a soda. You might select a muffin instead of a cookie or doughnut, but many muffins are high in fat, calories, and sugar. If you decide to eat a salad drenched in a high-fat dressing and topped with cheese instead of having a sandwich, you could be better off with the sandwich.

It's not easy to choose healthy foods when so many deceptive but unhealthy choices surround you.

You may be young and robust today, but statistics don't lie. A poor diet increases your risk of heart disease, diabetes, cancer, obesity, and many other illnesses. The food you eat is one of the biggest factors in how you *feel* every day. When you feel sluggish, you might assume you need sleep when what you may need is energizing food.

There is a reason we need to eat, and it isn't simply for convenience, speed, or pleasure. The more "real" food you eat, the more "real" you will feel. Select food that is *grown,* not processed. Eat food that is *fresh,* not from a can, cellophane package, or a box. You don't have to be a vegetarian to be healthy; you need protein and can eat meat, poultry, and fish if you want, but the bulk of your diet should include lots of fresh fruits and vegetables, raw nuts, and whole grains.

The correlation between diet and health is proven. Don't wait until you become ill to think about the food you eat. Appreciate and preserve your health. Enjoy the pleasures of eating, but if you are living to eat, reverse that and start eating to *live*. Only good things will happen as a result.

TIP # 67
Deal with problems.

Problems are inevitable, but few are insurmountable. Some people struggle with their problems more than others. It may be easier to avoid your problems, but they never really go away unless you face them. It takes courage and discipline to tackle the problems you encounter. Are you up to the challenge?

How do you deal with problems?

- **Do you view problems negatively?** Problems aren't always a bad thing. The process of working through a problem can improve relationships, reduce stress, stimulate new ways of thinking, and produce positive changes. Confronting someone about a problem does not have to be unpleasant or combative. View problems as challenges and catalysts for change. Every problem you face can teach you something new about yourself. Every problem can become an opportunity to expand your thinking, to learn, and to become a better, more compassionate person.

- **Do you dwell on your problems?** Obsessing about a problem and becoming fixated on it will not resolve it. In fact, it can do the opposite; the more you focus on what's wrong, the more you make out of it. Many problems can be easily resolved but instead are blown out of proportion. If you can't get your mind off a problem, the real issue may be your reaction. Focus on finding solutions. Look for the lessons to be learned and ways to move past your fixation on the problem.

● **Do you ignore your problems?** Ignoring a problem will not make it go away. You may be able to push it aside temporarily, but chances are it will surface again. Identify the reasons you prefer to ignore your problems. Are you leery of conflict, hurting someone's feelings, or being wrong? Consider that whatever it is you're trying to avoid could be the reason you're having the problem in the first place.

● **Do you blame others for your problems?** If you have a problem with someone or something, it is your problem, not theirs. Take responsibility for your contribution to the problems you have; own your problems. Blaming others for your troubles perpetuates the problem. Be the example of how you want others to be. Work at resolving your problems and forgiving others.

Every problem you face is an opportunity for you to do one of two things: Become a better person or let the problem get the best of you. You can acknowledge your problems or wait for someone else to do so. You can be solution-oriented or problem-oriented—the choice is yours.

TIP # 68
Set aside time for yourself.

Your plate is full. You've got a job to do, obligations to fulfill, commitments to keep, friends to see, and goals to accomplish. There are days you wish you could slow down enough to catch your breath, sit down to an enjoyable meal, or get to bed at a reasonable hour. And when someone suggests you set aside some time for yourself each day, you might wonder exactly how you're supposed to do that.

As your responsibilities increase, your time alone decreases. If you don't pay attention, you can lose your sense of self in your work and close relationships. When the majority of your time is spent working and your free time is spent socializing, you'll have little (if any) time left over for *you*.

Time won't stop or suddenly become available. You'll never *find* time to do the things you want to do; you must *schedule time* for the things that are most important to you. You need to make *yourself* a top priority. It isn't selfish to take time for yourself; it is essential to your overall well-being. Whether you set aside a few minutes or hours, the time you set aside for you is *yours*. It's your time to unwind, your time to think, and your time to do *whatever* you choose to do. If you don't set aside time for yourself and make it a priority, who will?

Set aside time to unplug and unwind. Unplug the phone, the television, the computer, and even the clock. When you unplug outside distractions, you will be able to plug into yourself. Take some time each day to get away from all the busyness and noise you've become accustomed to. Instead, use that time to listen to your thoughts. The more time you have the better, but if ten minutes is all you have, you can still unplug and unwind.

Set aside time to get *wet*. Take a long, hot shower. Soak in a bubble bath. Take a sauna, go swimming, walk barefoot on the beach, dangle your feet in a lake or a pool, or sit by a pond. Water is soothing, refreshing, and relaxing; look for ways to enjoy it.

Set aside time to put up a sign. Close your door and put out a DO NOT DISTURB sign. Request that others honor your time alone. Use this time to read, write, listen to music, or anything else you want to do.

Set aside time to *move*. Move your body. Go for a walk, a run, or a bike ride. Rollerblade, ice skate, or go for a swim. Walk around the mall and go shopping. It doesn't matter what you do as long as you are able to *move*. Exercise is essential—especially if you sit most of the day.

Set aside time to *read*. Go to the library, spend time in a bookstore, or create a reading nook in your home. Read in the tub, read in the sun, or read for fun. Read to think, read to learn, read to relax, or read to fall asleep. Whatever you do, read something you *enjoy*.

Set aside time to *sleep*. You need your rest. Depriving yourself of sleep negatively affects your physical health and mental clarity. Go to bed a little earlier. Snuggle up with a good book or magazine, watch your favorite television show, listen to music, or turn out the lights and go to sleep.

Set aside time to develop good habits. Make a habit of treating yourself well. Setting aside time for yourself should be a top priority. No matter how busy you are, never become too busy to take some time each day to do something special just for *you*. Even if it's only 15 minutes a day, you deserve at least that much.

TIP # 69
Freshen up!

After spending several days in bed sick with the flu, I was run down and exhausted. All I wanted was to stay in bed, but I knew I had to get up. People were counting on me. I had a speech to give. I dragged myself out of bed and moved in slow motion. It took me twice as long as usual to wash and dry my hair and put myself together.

When I was finally ready to walk out the door, I felt like a different person. Considering just an hour before I was barely able to move or speak, I was amazed at my own transformation. Not only did I look much healthier, but I felt healthier too. As the day progressed, I felt more and more alive and like my usual self.

If I hadn't had to give a speech that day, I would have stayed in bed. If I had stayed in bed, I am certain I would have felt as lethargic all day as I did that morning. I am convinced that getting up and *freshening up* was the medicine I needed. Getting out of bed and out of my sick clothes and into the shower and my professional clothes helped me begin to heal and feel like my usual self.

We all have good days and bad days. Some mornings, you might be so tired you'll decide to forgo your morning routine. You might decide to hit the snooze button instead of taking time to shave, wash and dry your hair, or iron your shirt. If you look a little grungy, you'll probably tell yourself how you look doesn't (and shouldn't) matter. *But it does.*

Good personal hygiene is important. Basic grooming habits are important. You should bathe, use deodorant, and brush and floss your teeth *every day.* Your hair, undergarments, and clothing should be washed *frequently.* When you take care of yourself, it will show. You will look good, feel good, and *smell* good.

Create a freshen-up kit and keep it in your car or desk at work for the times when you are on the go. Include some of the following items along with any others you can think of:

- Comb, brush, hairspray

- Toothbrush, toothpaste, toothpicks, and floss

- Mouthwash, mints, breath spray or drops

- Razor and shave cream

- Stain remover pads

- Sticky lint remover or lint brush

- Static remover spray

- Sewing kit and safety pins

- Scissors, nail clipper, and nail file

- Mirror

    Extra pair of socks or pantyhose

    Extra tie, shirt, or blouse

    Extra undergarments

    Cloth for wiping shoes or spills

    Hand sanitizer

    Tissue

    Make-up and make-up remover

    Nail polish (use to touch up nails or stop a run in your nylon)

    Umbrella

Be fresh and stay fresh. Take time each day to freshen up!

TIP # 70
Plan your day.

Setting goals is important; you need to identify the things you want and create a plan for your future. But don't overlook small, short-term goals. Your long-term success is a result of the things you do every day. Progress is a *process*. Setting goals and knowing what you want isn't enough to achieve it. You must have a plan and follow that plan. What you *do* each day will either move you closer to your goals or prevent you from reaching them.

Some of the best advice I ever received came out of a time-management seminar I took many years ago. In addition to learning how to use a planner, which I still carry with me today, I learned how to *plan*. I realized planning involves more than writing down appointments and coming up with a list of things to do. Making a plan and *sticking to that plan* is the key, although it's not as easy as it seems. Planning isn't difficult to do, but doing the things you plan can be quite a challenge.

We all have lots of things we want to do. The problem is that most of us have more things to do than time to do them. People are busy, but they are not always doing what they *should* be doing. Keeping busy can keep you from seeing what's happening to your time. If you try to do *everything*, you may end up accomplishing *nothing*. Every time you decide to do a random, unplanned task, you lose your focus and take time away from all the things you have planned.

When you take the time to *plan* your day, you will be more focused. You'll know what you need to do, and you'll spend your time *doing* the most vital things. As a result, you will be more productive and increase your chances of achieving your dreams.

Plan your day every day:

Stop *thinking* and start *planning*. *Thinking* is different from *planning*. A thought is an idea, and ideas come and go. We can think about something we'd like to do but may never get around to doing it. When an idea becomes more than a passing thought and you decide to do something with it, you've made a decision—a *plan* to do it. A thought is intangible, a plan concrete; ideas are temporary. Unless you capture them and put them into action, you won't benefit from them.

Put it in writing. If you keep track of your appointments and the things you need to do in your *head*, it's time to put them someplace else. Take your pick; whether you use an electronic or paper planner, either one is better than storing information in your memory. You may be quite capable of remembering, but there's no reason to add that pressure to your plans. Use your head, but use it to put things in writing.

Expect the unexpected. We seem so surprised when caught off guard. Traffic gets congested, the printer jams, packages don't arrive, computers stall, emergencies occur, and people get sick. We know anything can happen at any time. Why, then, are we so surprised when it does? The next time you schedule an appointment or meeting, block out extra time before it starts and after it is over. Don't be caught by surprise when traffic comes to a halt or someone has messed up your schedule—*expect and plan* for delays. Leave extra time in your schedule. When you expect the unexpected, you'll be prepared and able to deal with it because it won't be unexpected after all.

Keep information where you need it. People waste a lot of time looking for things. There's nothing more frustrating than needing information but not finding it. You will save time and reduce stress if you remember to keep information where you need it. When you schedule an appointment, write down the phone number, directions, and any other pertinent information in the same place you are writing the appointment. If you don't have enough room to write it there, be sure to reference where it is so you will be able to find it when you need it.

Plan one day at a time. Think about what you want and need to accomplish each day. Don't worry about all of the things you need or want to do this week, next month, or in three years. Focus on what you need to do *today*.

Underplan. Plan realistically and set yourself up to succeed. Be generous with your time when you plan your day; plan *extra* time for every task and appointment you have. Most people underestimate the amount of time it takes to get something done and then run out of time. Plan for interruptions and delays—make a plan you can follow that will help you get the most important things done. If you end up with little gifts of time between tasks, use that time for yourself.

Know your plan. A plan doesn't do you much good if you don't know what it is. Take time each morning to plan your day. See how much of your time is committed and how much is left over. Think about the things you'd *like* to do, and then decide what *must* be done. Put your thoughts into action and writing; use a paper or electronic planner to express what's in your head. Know where you need to be and what you need to do. You won't be able to follow a plan if you don't know what the plan is.

When you take the time to plan your day, you increase your focus and become more productive. You know what needs to be done and can spend your time doing it. As a result, you have more control over what you do each day and no longer feel that your days are controlling you. *Plan your day every day!*

TIP # 71
Avoid toxic people and environments.

I regretted answering the phone. I didn't have time for a long talk, but with this particular person our conversations always went on longer than I wanted. I was thrilled when I heard a knock at my door and my dog started barking. My caller heard it too, and we both knew I had to hang up the phone.

I greeted my neighbor and thanked her for coming to the door and helping me escape from what would have been a long and dreaded phone conversation. Her response surprised me. "You need to do a little housecleaning," she said. Before I could respond, she made it clear she thought my house looked fine. "I'm talking about the woman on the phone. If she has worn out her welcome, why do you keep inviting her in?"

My neighbor's advice sounded a bit harsh at first, but it did make sense. She got me to think about the "stuff" that was creating a "mess" in my life. I thought about the people I wanted in my "house" and those I could do without. Why did I give so much time to someone when it created so much stress? If someone came calling, I let that person into my life, but worse yet, I kept knocking myself out trying to be a perfect host!

When someone adds more stress to my life than I can handle and I feel uncomfortable around that person, I need to evaluate what the relationship means to me. I barely have even enough time for the people I *do* want in my life. I must decide whom I want to spend time with rather than allowing other people to make such important decisions for me.

Do you allow toxic people in *your* life? If you aren't sure, find out. Ask yourself the following questions.

Am I choosing to be with this person out of habit or convenience? People tend to spend time with the people they work with, live by, and or share common interests with. Would you go out of your way or travel a distance just to be with this person? If not, do you have a real friendship or one of convenience?

Do I feel good about myself when I am with this person? Does he or she treat you respectfully? Does this person try to change you, criticize you, or control you? Pay attention to how you *feel* around this person. A healthy relationship feels good—a toxic relationship can literally make you feel ill.

Do I want to spend time with this person? Who initiates your get-togethers? Does this person want to spend time with you, but you don't feel the same way? If you are responding to someone else's desire to spend time together, make sure you want to spend time together too.

Are my needs being met? Are you giving and giving without getting anything in return? Are your needs important to the relationship, or do they take a back seat to the needs of someone else? Do you have a voice in the relationship, feel listened to, and cared about? Not all relationships are split 50/50. It's fine to give more than you get as long as you choose to have it that way. But if you give and *hope* you'll get something back, or spend the majority of your time meeting the needs of others, you're likely neglecting your own needs. You deserve to get something back. Your needs are important too.

Does this person have qualities I look for in a friend? What qualities do you look for in a friend? Does this person possess these qualities? Are you proud to call this person your friend? Does he or she fit in and get along with your family and friends?

Do you look forward to his or her calls and your time together? Or do you try to avoid this person and make up excuses to avoid being with him or her? If you don't see qualities you value in someone, why do you keep this person as a friend?

Am I being too nice? In the preceding account, I talked on the phone with my "friend" because *she* wanted to; I held back *my* opinion because she wouldn't listen, and I allowed her to monopolize my time. I didn't want to hurt her, so I tried to be nice but ended up hurting myself in the process.

Am I willing to work at the relationship? Good relationships take time and effort but shouldn't drain you emotionally or leave you feeling frustrated. Is this person important enough to you to work at improving the relationship? If you don't care enough about someone to make the relationship better, you probably don't need the relationship.

Is this a toxic relationship? If you are unhappy with the way someone treats you or talks to you, or if you feel stuck and hope things will change, think seriously about why you stay in the relationship. If someone hurts you physically or emotionally by yelling, blaming, shaming, teasing, scolding, smothering, or controlling you, you are in a toxic relationship. Toxic relationships can destroy you. Reevaluate the relationship. You have options. Talk with someone who can help you, and consider seeking professional help.

Beware of toxic people, relationships, and environments. A person can be good *to* you yet not good *for* you. Whether at work, home, or somewhere else, pay attention to the way you *feel* around other people. Do a little housekeeping; clean out the "stuff" that's either "messing" with you or *messing you up*.

TIP # 72
Keep a journal.

Journaling is good for your health. The simple act of putting your thoughts on paper is highly therapeutic. You don't have to be a good writer to journal. You don't have to worry about what to say. You don't have to read what you write to get the benefit, nor allow anyone else to read it either. So why bother journaling at all?

Why Journal?

If you're not sure journaling is something you want to do, consider its many benefits. Journaling can help you:

Relax and reduce stress.

Improve your mental and emotional health.

Face and get over your fears.

Resolve your problems.

Express your feelings, identify emotional and physical triggers, and understand yourself better.

Keep track of information, experiences, and events.

Improve your mood.

Increase your mental clarity.

Expand your creativity.

Manage and adjust to change.

You can journal as often as you want. You can do it anytime and anywhere. You don't have to worry about the way your writing looks; forget about sentence structure, spelling, and grammar. You can scribble, doodle, or draw. The process is more important than the content. Write a letter to yourself or to someone else. Write a story or a poem or make a list. There is no right or wrong way to journal. Your journal is yours alone, so you get to decide what to do with it.

You can buy a fancy book, use a scrap of paper, or use your computer. Just put your pen to the paper or your fingers to the keyboard and let yourself go. It gets easier over time. Clear your mind, think through your thoughts, get in touch with your feelings. Keep a log of your life, and leave a legacy for future generations. You decide.

TIP # 73
Smoke and booze; you lose.

Cigarette and alcohol advertisements feature young, vibrant, attractive models drinking, smoking, and socializing. They are surrounded by friends and lovers, and their sparkling smiles radiate happiness and good times. If advertising doesn't convince you that you'll look good and have fun if you smoke and drink, walk into any hot spot, be it a nightclub, bar, or restaurant, and you'll see a similar scene: young and vibrant people smoking (when and where permitted), drinking, smiling, and laughing.

If you are on the outside looking in, you might think you are viewing the "winners" in life. The message: Smoke and go on a drinking binge and you *win*.

You might decide you're a loser and wish you were meeting more people and having more fun. You might decide you feel better when you drink and more confident when you smoke. In fact, you might end up getting so much smoke in your eyes that you won't even see you are *changing*. And when you finally do take notice of the changes, you might not even recognize the person you see.

There is a downside to this "beautiful" life, and there is nothing pretty about it. Smoking and drinking are two of the most destructive habits people have. There are many misconceptions about the effects of both and many reasons why so many people do them. Do you see your reasons for smoking or drinking in any of these eight common rationales?

1. **Smoking is cool.** If you think smoking is cool, smoke a cigarette outside the doorway of a building, and observe the reactions (and sneers) of the people who have to walk through your cloud of smoke to enter.

2. **Smoking makes me look older.** If you think smoking will make you look older, it will. It won't take long for wrinkles to appear, and you will age prematurely and much faster than your nonsmoking friends.

3. **Drinking and smoking help me relax.** If you think drinking will relax you or a cigarette will calm your nerves, the affect will only be short-term. You will be on a vicious cycle. Your need to smoke and drink will increase and could become an addiction or worse.

4. **Drinking helps me forget my problems.** If you think drinking will enable you to forget your small problems, it might but only because your drinking will create bigger problems to worry about.

5. **Drinking helps me feel less self-conscious.** If you think drinking will help you feel less self-conscious and make you more socially acceptable, consider that chances are good you'll do something stupid under the influence of alcohol, embarrass yourself, and feel even more uncomfortable as a result.

6. **Smoking and drinking will make me feel better.** If you think smoking or drinking will make you feel better, consider that you'll be trading one ailment for another. The short-term high you get is likely to result in a lower low when your addiction kicks in.

7. **Smoking and drinking will make me one of the beautiful people.** If you think smoking or drinking will make you more attractive, it won't. There's nothing attractive about stained teeth or yellow nails, tobacco or alcohol breath, or a person unable to walk a straight line or speak without slurring his or her words.

8. **Society expects social drinking.** If you think you will be ostracized if you don't drink, you won't. It wasn't neces-

sary to go along with the crowd when you were young, and it isn't as you age. Be true to yourself and don't feel pressure to conform.

The truth about smoking and drinking:

Smoking and drinking are addicting. You may tell yourself you'll be able to quit when you want, but quitting is extremely difficult.

Smoking and drinking are expensive. The amount you pay and how much you consume will only increase over time. The longer you indulge, the more money you throw away.

Smoking and drinking are bad for your health. Drinking and smoking increase your risk of numerous diseases, shortening your life span.

Smoking and drinking are dangerous. Drinking and driving is lethal, smoking is hazardous, and both are harmful to you and others.

Smoking and drinking affect your relationships. When your addiction is your focus and becomes more important than your friends and family, your relationships will suffer.

There's nothing good about smoking or drinking. It's easy to think you have your smoking or drinking under control, but that only means you don't realize when your habit starts controlling you.

If you don't smoke, don't start. If you do smoke, quit now, before more damage is done. And if you drink, drink sparingly or go without alcohol awhile to make sure you can. You might even find you feel better when you do. And if you think you have a drinking problem, admit it. You have lots of company. Don't be ashamed to feel powerless or unable to kick a smoking or drinking habit. Admitting dependency is one of the first steps in overcoming an addiction. You can do it.

TIP # 74

Learn how to de-stress.

Everyone experiences stress. Some people say life is more stressful today than ever before. Health care providers say stress-related disorders are on the rise. Approximately 75 percent of all doctor visits are thought to be stress-related. Stress can be a motivator, but when mild stress turns into chronic or severe stress, it's time to do something about it.

- If you have frequent headaches or stomach aches, tight muscles, a bad back, or catch more than your share of colds or the flu, it could be due to stress.

- If you feel tired but cannot get to sleep or if you feel edgy, more irritable than usual, or sensitive and moody, it could be stress-related.

- If your relationships become strained and people make more demands or seem needier, it could be their reaction to your stress.

- If traffic seems heavier, the days longer or shorter, the boss more demanding, or coworkers more bothersome, it's likely from stress.

- If you feel overcommitted, have trouble keeping track of appointments, fall behind schedule, or forget important information, the culprit probably is stress.

- If your motivation is down, your anxiety is up, and you're smoking or drinking more but eating less and less, the problem is most likely your stress.

- If you're eating on the run, your gas tank is empty, your bills are overdue, and your house is a mess, its stress.

- If you have no time to yourself but bend over backwards for everyone else, you pass the stress test.

Pay attention to triggers of stress and learn how to *de-stress* when stress hits. More important, do everything you can to prevent stress in your life. There are many ways to help counter and prevent stress. Incorporate as many as you can into your daily routine.

Here are 20 things you can do to make sure stress doesn't get the best of you:

1. Exercise. Stretch, do yoga, walk, run, or just move.

2. Eat a healthy, well-balanced diet. Drink less caffeine and more water.

3. Get enough sleep. Try going to bed and waking up at the same time every day.

4. Take breaks.

5. Listen to relaxing music.

6. Breathe deeply.

7. Express your emotions.

8. Meditate and visualize.

9. Resolve your problems.

10. Delegate or ask for help.

11. Say no. Don't take on more than you can handle.

12. Laugh.

13. Stick to a budget and reduce your debt.

14. Get organized.

15. Forgive yourself and others.

16. Create a relaxing environment.

17. Focus on one day at a time.

18. Pray.

19. Let go of your need to control.

20. Have fun.

Take charge of your time and your life. If you fail to control your stress, your stress will end up controlling you.

TIP # 75
No more excuses.

Excuses. Excuses. Excuses. We make them, we give them, and we accept them. It's not easy to say, "I made a mistake," "I don't know how," "I won't," or "I can't." It's easier to avoid the truth, prevent an argument, and explain our failures away.

We make excuses to preserve our relationships. We make excuses to save ourselves time. We make excuses to avoid hurting people or making someone mad. We make excuses for our lack of commitment and follow through. We make excuses because we're lazy or didn't do what we were supposed to do. We make excuses for other people, and sometimes we make excuses for our excuses!

Do you make excuses?

Do you frequently apologize? How often do you say, "I'm sorry; I didn't mean to"?

Do you blame others? Do you frequently place the fault on someone else?

Do you blame circumstances? How often are you delayed in traffic, have emergencies, or encounter unusual extenuating circumstances? And how frequently do these things become the reason you did or didn't do something?

Do you blame yourself? Do you negate your abilities? Are you too quick to take the blame when things go wrong?

Do you lack confidence? Do you doubt your ability? Have you stopped trying or do you give up too easily?

Do you justify your reasons? Do you rationalize your decisions and give long, unnecessary explanations?

Do you give up easily? Are you a quitter, do you lack will-power, or fail to see things through?

Do you keep your word? Do you frequently change your mind or break promises you've made?

No one is perfect and you don't have to try to be. It's okay to slip up every now and then. There will be times when you let yourself and others down. Admit it when you've made a mistake. Be up front and tell someone when you are upset or unable to follow through. If you don't have a reason, don't make up one. Simply apologize, but remember that saying "I'm sorry" does not justify whatever you did

Be honest with yourself and others; don't sugarcoat the truth. The only acceptable excuse is no excuse at all!

TIP # 76
Turn off the lights.

I've been living on my own for over 25 years and am self-suffi-cient. Yet anytime I am sick, I think about calling my *mom*. I know she can provide whatever I need, be it food, medicine, or advice. I could and should rely on myself for these things, but it's tempt-ing to relinquish my responsibility to someone else.

Think about the times you acted irresponsibly. When you lived at home, if you didn't remember to take out the garbage, walk the dog, or mow the lawn, someone was there to remind you. If you failed to turn out the lights, turn off the iron, or turn on the alarm, someone else was there to do it for you.

Did you hear reminders often? Do you think your parents were trying to irritate you by nagging you? Think again. They knew the day would come when they would no longer be there to look after you, and they were only trying to *teach* you responsibility.

As an adult, you must look after yourself. You are free to do whatever you want. You can leave clothes on the floor and dirty dishes in the sink, and you can let garbage pile up if you want. No one will care (except maybe your spouse or roommate). But if you forget to lock the door or blow out the candles, you're putting yourself *and others* in jeopardy.

Your adult responsibilities go beyond taking care of yourself; you share the responsibility with billions of others to make the world a better place. Consider the effect your actions have on the environment and other people. As a responsible citizen, do what you can to help conserve energy, reduce waste, and stop pollution.

No one will notice if you fail to turn off the lights. It's up to you to notice. Do it because you want to live responsibly, not because someone tells you to.

Don't feel as though you need to do something big; it's the little things you do each day that help restore and save the planet and will prevent bigger problems in the future.

Turn out the lights. You really don't need to have every light in the house on when you are watching TV in one room. Conserve energy and save yourself some money. Get into the habit of turning on the light when you enter a room and turning it off every time you leave a room.

Don't shave in the shower. Even the finest hotels are encouraging guests to conserve. Fix the leaky faucet, repair the running toilet, and wait to wash your jeans until you have additional clothes to put in the washing machine. When you shave in the shower you are wasting running water. So turn the shower off when you shave, or make the decision to shave someplace else.

Lock up. Lock the doors and windows, both when you're at home and when you leave. An open window on the first floor or in the basement is an invitation for anyone to enter. There are ways to be safe and secure without being cooped up. Most police and fire departments will be happy to send someone out to your home or apartment to give you suggestions for making your home safe.

Make your bed. Even though you plan on unmaking it again in a few more hours, make your bed; you'll sleep better if you do. A freshly made bed is inviting, and taking the time to make it is habit-forming. When you get out of bed in the morning, make it right away. It doesn't take long and will set the tone for a well-structured and organized day.

Hang up your towel. It takes only a few seconds, but take the time to hang up your towel and you'll see how much faster it will dry. Don't wash it—use it again and again. When you use a towel to dry off after a shower, you and the towel are *clean*. Why wash a towel every time you use it? How dirty can it get when you use it only to wipe yourself dry?

Reset your thermostat. In the winter, you will be cold. In the summer, you will be hot. Dress accordingly. There is no sense wearing a heavy winter sweater in the middle of the summer because the thermostat is set so low. Set it to be comfortable. Consider its harmful effects on the environment and on your finances.

Reuse and recycle. Recycle your newspapers, bottles, containers, and cans. Do your part to prevent excess waste. Drink from a reusable cup instead of from a new paper cup that you throw away. Buy larger, value items rather than the more expensive and smaller items. There are tons of waste polluting our environment—don't add more than absolutely necessary.

Choose conservation over convenience. Walk to the store; don't drive. Take public transportation. Join a car pool. Ride a bike. Run your errands methodically—don't drive all over the place. Think about our dependence on oil, the price of gas, and the problems from pollution. Then think about alternative ways to get where you're going.

Turn everything *off.* If it's been turned on, turn it off. Turn off your curling iron, turn off your computer, and turn off the coffee pot. Blow out candles and remember clothes dryers can cause fire too. Always look things over before you leave a room, go to sleep, or leave for the day, and get into the habit of turning everything off.

Over time you will remember the things your parents told you to do. If you become a parent, you'll tell your children many of the same things your parents told you. You won't do it to bother them; you'll do it because you *care.* You'll want to *protect and*

educate your children in the same way your parents tried to protect and educate you.

TIP # 77

Guard your shadow; it follows you wherever you go.

The time to start building and protecting your reputation is *now*.

You already know it's important to take care of yourself,
because your physical and emotional health is essential to your
well-being and ability to perform well. If you care about your
health, you'll live a healthful lifestyle. If you want to stay close to
your family and friends, you'll stay in contact with them. If success is important to you, you'll develop habits that lead to success.
Thus, it follows that if you want to ensure your reputation is positive, you'll think about the things you do.

Your reputation is a result of everything you do—or don't do. Like
a shadow, your reputation follows you wherever you go. You might
not think the things you do today will matter years from now, but
they will. Your character and integrity are at the core of your being.

You've seen it happen in politics: Candidates running for public
office are scrutinized. Any wrongdoing or questionable behavior in
someone's past can be brought to the forefront. Candidates' dreams
have been shattered when scrutiny has uncovered their indiscre-
tions. When the media and opposing political parties are determined to tarnish someone's reputation, they will stop at nothing,
unless there's nothing in the person's past to use against them.

Even outside the political scene, your reputation follows you
wherever you go. You won't have to look over your shoulder or
have anything to worry about if you cultivate a reputation to be
proud of. Decide what kind of reputation you want and what kind
of person you want to be. Then live your life accordingly. *Think*
about your reputation today and in the future.

Think about the kind of person you want to be. Think about the
qualities that are most important to you. What characteristics do

you want or need to work on? If you want to be a good person, what does "good" mean to you? How will you know if you are the person you want to be? Think about the way you want others to see you, and think about the way you see yourself. You can be the person you want to be.

Think about the things you *say*. Do you say hurtful things you later regret? Do you put people down, minimize someone's feelings, or lash out in anger? Saying "I'm sorry" is important but only when it is sincere. Even if you apologize, words can sting, and people may become leery of you. The more frequently you apologize, the less impact your apology will have. If you want to be viewed as a rational, thoughtful person, think about the things you say. When you choose your words carefully you'll have fewer regrets and won't spend time worrying (or wondering) about what you've said.

Think about the things you *do*. Your actions, not your *intentions*, matter most. What you *do* is what people remember. You can *tell* someone how important he or she is to you, but if you don't spend time with that person, your words are meaningless. You can *say* you're ambitious, but if you're not working hard, no one will believe you. Your actions reveal your *true* feelings. Do more and say less. Actions really do speak louder than words.

Think about the commitments you make. If you say you'll be there, be there. If you say you'll get something done, get it done. If you say you'll call, you'd better call. You are better off not committing than offering to do something but failing to follow through. Your words belong to you; you choose what you say you'll do. Until you give others a reason to doubt you, they will be counting on you and believing in you. Every commitment you make but break, no matter how small, damages your reputation. Don't overcommit, and be sure to honor the commitments you make.

Think about your limitations. You are human and can do only so much. If you try to be perfect or try to please everyone else, you'll end up disappointing others as well as yourself. Be realistic about the things you can do and have time to do. Think about what happens when you let yourself and others down. If you frequently fall behind or fail to accomplish what you set out to do, either someone is expecting too much of you or you are expecting too much of yourself. Know, accept, and handle your limitations.

Think about the way you treat other people. Do you treat everyone respectfully and courteously? Or do you give special treatment and pay extra attention only to those you think can help you? Do you choose your friends based on the qualities they possess or based on what you think they can do for you? Do you spend more time "buttering up" the boss than getting to know your coworkers? All people have value; when you fail to treat all people well, even those you do favor will notice. Besides, the person you bypass today could end up being someone you need something from tomorrow. Treat all people well.

Some things may seem so small that you brush them off as insignificant, but it can be a big mistake. Your reputation is built over time, and the seemingly insignificant things determine your reputation.

Be on the lookout; think about your reputation every time you choose your words, your deeds, and your actions. Everything you do and say will follow you wherever you go, just like a shadow. Guard yourself. Guard your shadow. Be the person you want to be by living your life purposefully.

TIP # 78
Be your own best friend.

Have you ever had a *best* friend? It's fun to have a best friend, especially when the friendship lasts. I had a best friend who lived across the street from me. We were very young when we decided we would be best friends *forever.* I felt more secure knowing I had a best friend; it was nice to have someone I could count on. Our friendship was strong, spanning high school and college, but our friendship was put to the test when we went our separate ways as adults. When my best friend married, everything changed. She couldn't be there for me the way she had before, which I understood, but it left a void in my life. I had other friends, but no one replaced my best friend—until I met my husband.

My husband and I spent as much time as we could together when we were dating and after we married. Over the years, our lives changed and our responsibilities grew, and we found less and less time to spend together. There were times I needed my husband when he simply wasn't available. I had other friends, but they were busy managing their own hectic lives. I no longer could depend on others; I knew I needed to depend on myself.

No one can do for me what I need to do for myself. I like knowing my husband will be there when I need him and feel good having friends who care, but I no longer *depend* on them.

What is a friend, after all? A good friend should be a bonus, not an obligation. I don't want to be a burden to my friends with every little problem I have—I want to *enjoy* my friends and want them to enjoy being with me. If you expect someone to be there all the time, you might end up disappointed. The older you get, the more you will see how busy everyone can be. It's not that your friends don't *want* to be there for you; sometimes they just *can't* be there for you. Instead of relying on everyone else, you need to rely on yourself.

The best thing to do is to be your own best friend. Develop a relationship with *yourself*. Depend on yourself. When you need to work something through, take some time to be with you. When you have a strong friendship with yourself, you will have better friendships with everyone else because you won't be so needy with your friends. When you're not a burden but are an easygoing friend, you're the very best kind of friend for others to have.

TIP # 79
Trust your instincts.

You can call it what you want: a gut feeling, a premonition, or just a hunch. You might refer to it as your intuition, your inner wisdom, your conscience, or that little voice you hear in your head. At times you may think you're being silly and try to ignore the feelings you have. Relying on your instincts is not something most of us have been encouraged to do.

- Have you ever had a strong feeling about something yet no basis for the feeling you felt?

- Have you ever felt ill when there was nothing physically wrong?

- Have you ever felt anxious for no apparent reason or had a feeling too vague to explain?

- Have you ever suddenly thought about someone right before the phone rang, only to find that person calling you?

- Have you ever had a song on your mind moments before it played on the radio?

- Have you ever had a premonition about something before it happened?

- Have you ever had a dream that came true?

- Have you ever lost your energy around certain people?

- Have you ever wavered about a decision you had to make?

- Have you ever felt uneasy about someone or something but didn't know why?

If any of these things have happened to you, your intuition has been in touch with you. Some of the things you consider coincidences may not be as much of a fluke as you assume. Pay attention to the subtle and not-so-subtle signs you receive; you may be more intuitive than you think. Learn to discover the ways in which your intuition communicates with you. It might be a feeling, thought, or physical or emotional sensation. Whatever it is, it's too important to ignore.

Children are naturally intuitive, and chances are at one time you were too. Children trust their feelings until they are conditioned to *think* instead of *feel*. When you were young and afraid, you didn't have to deny your fears. If you didn't trust someone, you could run and hide; you weren't compelled to conceal the way you felt about someone. As you matured, you didn't want to appear foolish, so you (and everyone else) learned to deny such feelings.

If you've ever had a bad feeling you've dismissed as irrational, you were working *against* your intuition. Start working with your intuition instead. Your instincts can *protect* you. Your initial reaction is always your best safety measure. If something seems odd, it probably is.

Trust your feelings; how you feel *does* matter. Allow your instincts to alert you to dangerous situations, prevent you from making mistakes, and guide you in making important decisions. Don't argue with your intuition. If something or someone doesn't feel right, there's a good chance something could go wrong.

Your feelings are not right or wrong. Don't try to justify the way you feel. Let your feelings guide you. Trust your instincts.

TIP # 80
Get a tetanus shot.

I had an appointment with my doctor for my annual check up. As we caught up with each other, I told my doctor about the books I was writing. She has always enthusiastically supported my work and was exceptionally enthused about *this* book. She wanted to know all about the tips and made me promise to reserve a copy of the book for her. When we concluded the exam, she wished me well, and just as she was about to open the door and leave, she turned to me and said, "Tell them to be sure to get their tetanus shot." I half-heartedly agreed, thanked her for the idea, and said good-bye.

I was still in the development stages of my book, and although I wasn't sure if writing about health fit in with the concept, her advice stuck with me. It wasn't until my daughter developed a sinus infection that I saw my doctor again. After she checked my daughter, I asked her if she was serious about her idea for the tip "Get a tetanus shot." She was and I asked her to tell me more.

She explained how everyone should have a tetanus shot every ten years. By the time most people graduate, many will be due for a shot, but the last thing most people think about after graduation is going to the doctor. The more she explained, the more I understood the importance of this tip. "I want all the young, healthy people to stay healthy," she said.

Whether you're graduating from high school or college, you'll be busy preparing for and entering the next chapter of your life. Finding a place to live and work and starting a new job can be all consuming. You'll have even less free time once you are working full time. You'll no longer have yearly health forms to complete for school, and no one is going to make you an appointment for your annual checkup at the doctor or dentist. Your health is now in your hands, where it belongs.

Take good care of yourself. Don't wait until you are sick to see a doctor. Do it while you are healthy and increase your chances of staying that way. Prevention is the key.

Take charge of your health and take preventive health measures:

Find a doctor and a dentist. If you don't have one, ask around for recommendations.

Get annual check ups.

Brush and floss your teeth every morning, evening, and in between.

Eat a healthful, well-balanced diet.

Drink lots of purified water.

Limit your alcohol, caffeine, and sugar intake.

Maintain a weight consistent with your height and build.

Exercise.

Your long-term health is a result of the habits you develop today. Invest in yourself and your health. Do all of these things, and remember my doctor's advice. If you haven't done it yet, go and get a tetanus shot. Keep health records and get your tetanus shot every ten years or so.

TIP # 81

Invest in your future.

Let's talk about money. Do you think you manage your money well? Does money worry you or cause you stress? Do you wonder if you will have enough money to do the things you want, or do you assume you'll manage somehow? Do you control your spending, or does your spending control you?

Do you plan to own your own home someday? Do you want to buy a different car or a better computer? Will you ever need a new bed, furniture, or appliances? Do you foresee a lot of travel in your future? Do you know how much these things cost? Do you know what it will take for you to qualify for a mortgage or loan?

If you don't know all you need to know about money, you're not alone. The knowledge you need for a secure financial future is not included in the curriculum of most schools. Your ability to do the things you want and to live the lifestyle you choose is dependent not only on what you earn but on what you do with your earnings. If you spend everything you make, you will live paycheck to paycheck. If you invest wisely, you will watch your earnings grow.

Perhaps you've saved money and invested wisely over the years and will continue to do the same. If you are like most young adults today, however, you've freely spent the money you've had.

When you work full time and earn a bigger salary, you will have more money than you've had before. It will be exciting when you receive a big paycheck, but beware—the more you make, the more you will want to spend. Before you spend all you've got, think about the life you want to live. What you do with your money today will determine your lifestyle in the future.

This is an important time in your life. You are about to become a self-supporting adult, and your expenses are about to skyrocket. The big salary you are making isn't all it appears to be. The more you make, the more you will be taxed. The bigger your home, the higher your utility bills and property taxes will be.

Think about the things you want to achieve, accomplish, and accumulate. Become aware of the costs involved in the lifestyle you choose. Make plans and set goals, not just for the things you want to do but also for how you will afford to do these things.

Create and stick to a budget.

Live below, not above, your means.

Plan your purchases; avoid making impulsive purchases.

Pay with cash; charge only what you can pay for when the bill arrives.

Pay your bills on time.

Take advantage of 401K and employer-matched retirement funds.

Save your money; invest wisely.

If you aren't sure you know how to invest in your future, seek the advice of someone who does. Utilize the many resources available to help you. Find information on the Internet. Read books or consult financial experts. Take advantage of free services. The best source you have, however, is *you;* you are the one who will decide what you do with your money. Take control of your finances; don't let your finances control you. Invest in yourself; invest in your future.

Demonstrate a Positive Attitude

Make Your Life a Little Easier

TIP # 82

Your attitude is your choice.

One spring my family and I attended one graduation open house after another. It was a gloomy day, and although most of the events took place outside, some hosts had set up their garages and family rooms just in case the weather wouldn't cooperate. It didn't. By the time we arrived at the third open house, it began raining. The parents of the graduate hurriedly took down the outdoor set-up and squeezed everything into the garage, which was filled with bikes, toys, and tools. We barely had a chance to say hello before we helped the other guests carrying trays of food, tables, and chairs from the backyard into the garage. There was little room for all the people and the food, and the parents complained, blaming the weather for ruining the day.

I felt sorry for the parents, not only because the weather was bad but because they seemed so surprised. They had no alternate plan. They relied on the unpredictable weather, rather than on themselves, to make the party a success.

According to Petra Marquart, an authority on customer service and author of *The Power of Service,* other people can affect your mood in the same way the weather does. "Attitude," she says, "is the *emotional climate* in which we live." If you feel down at the end of each day or drained after spending time with friends, there's probably a reason. According to Marquart, it could be because you're working next to "drizzle" or hanging around "dark skies."

Anyone whose mood depends on other people, environmental factors, or other influences beyond their control is going to be unpredictable and unreliable. Imagine trying to have a meaningful relationship with such a person. It's not easy being around people whose moods change as quickly and frequently as the weather does.

No one can predict the weather with total accuracy, yet we follow forecasts and make our plans accordingly. When you plan an outdoor event or activity, you *hope* the weather will cooperate, but you know you shouldn't count on it. If you don't have an alternate plan or the flexibility to adapt, you shouldn't plan the event outside. The weather may be unpredictable, but your attitude doesn't have to be.

If the weather ruins your plans, you have a right to be disappointed. You can rant and rave, but no matter what you do, it won't change the weather. It didn't deliberately ruin your plans, and guess what? *The weather doesn't care.*

When it "rains on your parade," your parade isn't ruined unless *you* ruin it. Your *reaction* to the rain affects the outcome more than anything else. Of course you're let down, but you don't need to wallow in your sorrow. The rain may have dampened the *event*, but it doesn't have to dampen your *spirits*.

The weather is unpredictable; people are too. Don't rely on either to make you happy. You can *prefer* sunshine over rain or an easy-going coworker over a difficult one, but you will have to accept and deal with whatever you get.

You are not powerless. You can weather any storm. Be your own barometer. You choose your attitude—you control your response. Do you want to be a cloud of dread or a ray of sunshine? **You** decide; *your attitude is your choice.*

TIP # 83
Make someone's day.

Make someone's day. It's one of the simplest, most gratifying things you can do. There are countless ways to make someone's day. Start by looking for things you can do. There's no need to spend money or take up a lot of your time; it really is the little things that count. Make someone's day a little better, and you will find that your day is a little better too.

Seven ways to make someone's day:

1. *Acknowledge hard work and effort.* Sometimes you have to stay up late, get up early, and go out of your way to get something done. You feel good about the things you do, but it's nice when others notice too. You can do that for your coworkers. Do more than say "nice job"; acknowledge someone's dedication, efforts, and hard work. When you do, you can be sure you will make someone feel appreciated, and it will make his or her day.

2. *Offer encouragement.* A little push or an extra vote of confidence will help anyone in need. When someone else believes in you, it's easier for you to believe in yourself. When was the last time you offered your support or asked someone (and wanted to hear) how he or she was doing? How often have you said, "Keep it up; you're doing great. I know you'll make it?" Look around. Do you see someone losing hope? Does anyone seem afraid? Why not encourage that person? Your encouraging words can make a difference—they can *be* the difference between someone's failure and success. Offer your encouragement and you will surely make someone's day.

3. *Be there.* Be there for people. Be there for *their* needs, not yours. Be there to listen, and be there to share. Be there in good times, and be there in bad times. Be there to laugh, be there to cry, and be there to lend a helping hand. Be there to show you care; be there because you care. Be there because you *want* to, not because you *ought* to. When you are there for someone, you will make that person's day.

4. *Do something unexpectedly.* Pick up the check, hold open the door; send flowers, or deliver balloons. Bake chocolate chip cookies, make a lunch or reservations for dinner, make a big congratulation sign, or decorate the room with streamers. Do someone a favor, clean up someone's mess, pay someone a compliment, or leave a wrapped present on the desk. Send a card, or call to say hello. Wait patiently, listen calmly, or ask how someone feels. Do something simple yet thoughtful, but whatever you do, do it unexpectedly. When you do, you will make someone's day.

5. *Say it.* You know how you feel, you know what you think, and you know how much you care. But no one else will know unless you tell them so. If you think it, say it: "I enjoy being with you." "I'm proud of you." "I love you." "Thank you for being you." No one knows how you feel; no one can read your mind. If you have something to say, why not say it? When you do, you'll make someone smile, and you will know you've made someone's day.

6. *Pay attention.* Notice what you see. Notice what you hear. Notice *everyone* you see. Don't walk by; stop and say hello. Notice someone's haircut; notice the photo on the desk. Notice someone's positive outlook; notice when someone's upset. Notice when someone's excluded; notice when someone is ill. Pay attention to detail, for the more you notice, the more you'll see how very important paying attention can be. Pay attention. Make someone's day.

7. *Get excited.* Get excited, as excited as you'd be for yourself. Get excited for someone's promotion; celebrate when someone reaches a goal. Get excited over someone's new purchase; be happy for the money that person saved. Get excited about someone's vacation. Congratulate someone who gets a raise. Get excited about someone's good for-

tune. Get excited about someone's success. Get excited about making a habit of making someone's day *every* day.

TIP # 84
Believe in yourself.

The dance team had been through a rough season. Participating in one of the most competitive divisions in the state, they hadn't done as well as they had hoped. Their dream of representing their division at the state conference was slipping away.

The upcoming competition would determine which teams advance to the state level. The girls were excited about the dance they choreographed, but their confidence was waning. They wanted to do well, but they didn't think they had a chance.

Many of the dancer's parents (myself included) felt frustrated with what seemed to be biased judging inequities, but with little time to spare we realized even *our* attitudes needed adjusting. Up until now, our role was to raise money for the team. With just two weeks to go until the big competition, we knew no amount of money would help the situation.

The girls had the talent and ability to make it to state. The only thing missing was the *belief* they could. As members of the dance team booster club, we parents were determined to "boost" the girl's spirits and "raise" their thinking to a higher level.

We came up with a plan. Each day for the following two weeks, a group of parents showed up at practice to encourage and cheer the girls on. We knew the dance team could do well, and we told them so. We celebrated their effort with banners, posters, mementos, and pizza parties. We embarrassed them (and ourselves) as we entered the gym shaking pom-poms and noise makers.

We had serious moments with the girls too. We read inspirational stories and poems and all got together to watch a few movies about an underdog who becomes the champion. One day we surprised each girl with a copy of the book *The Little Engine That Could,* by Wally Piper. A classic children's tale, it reinforces the power of belief in oneself.

The story is about a little engine that manages to pull itself over the top of a steep mountain. The bigger engines that said "I cannot" watch as the little engine slowly pushes up the mountain while saying "I think I can—I think I can—I think I can" over and over. It became the dance-team mantra.

The girls were having fun again, and it showed when they danced. The competition day arrived, and right before they were about to perform, they huddled together to chant their new mantra.

Two weeks prior, going to state seemed impossible, and the team assumed they *could not* win. Everything changed when they changed their thinking. Once the girls realized they *could* do well, they **decided** they *would* do well. Because they believed in themselves and believed they would make it to state, they did.

The girls credit the parents, but the credit goes to the girls. Nothing we did could have helped unless the girls were willing to help themselves. The parents always believed the girls could win, but the girls' belief needed to come from within.

When you cast doubt on yourself, you create doubt in everyone else. When you believe in yourself, you won't need reassurance from anyone else. Instead of assuming you *can't*, why not assume you *can*?

If you believe you can't succeed, you probably won't. You are more likely to succeed when you believe you can. Your beliefs create your reality; you choose what you believe. You can believe in someone else but are much better off when you choose to believe in yourself.

TIP # 85
Consider yourself fortunate.

Most people fail to realize how fortunate they are until they no longer have what they should have been grateful for all along.

How often do you call the important people in your life to say hello or "I love you?" When was the last time you watched the sun rise—or set? Do you take time each day to stop and smell the roses? Do you appreciate the comforts of home, the food you eat, or any of the modern conveniences you've become accustomed to? Do you plop into bed too exhausted to give thanks for all you have? If you're too busy to think about how fortunate you are, *slow down.*

Gratitude is *good* for you. When you are grateful for what you have, you don't think about what you lack. When you are grateful for the little things as well as the big things, you add pleasure to your life. Sometimes it isn't until we lose the things or people we take for granted that we realize what we had. Absence really does make the heart grow fonder.

A friend of mine hadn't realized how fortunate he was until he was thousands of miles away from home. Being away from his daily routine provided him with ample time to *think*. He thought a lot about the things he missed the most and the lessons he was learning while he was away. When he returned home after serving his country at war, he sent a letter to his family and friends.

I was touched by what he wrote. It caused me to think about my own good fortune, about the things I take for granted, including my freedom, which people in some countries lack. I realized that my problems pale in comparison to the problems of others.

My friend gave me permission to share part of his letter. When you read it, I hope you, too, will stop and think about your own good fortune. No matter how big your problems may seem, there's a good chance you are more fortunate than you think. The following are a few of the lessons my friend, Command Sergeant Major Duane Fredrickson, learned while he was away:

● It's the little things in life that make a difference, like sunny side eggs (we only got the powdered version) or a Starbucks coffee.

- I learned the value of making the best of all situations. Rather than complain, I endeavored to find the positive and create fun.

- I gained an understanding of what it means to have nothing.

- I learned sand can reside in places you and I have never imagined; I took four showers in a row to rid myself of the dirt.

- I learned that roach motels will catch centipedes, crickets, and spiders as well as cockroaches that are four-inches long. (I put four of these motels around my bed and they filled up so quickly that I needed to replace them once a week.)

- I have a new appreciation of the true value of friendship and realize I've taken my friends for granted.

- I discovered at times I've taken those I love the most for granted too and realized how very important they are to me.

My friend traveled thousands of miles away from home to learn some of life's most valuable lessons. He is fortunate because he returned home safely and was able to share what he learned with others.

You don't have to travel far to realize how much you have to be grateful for. Some of the most important things in your life are right before your eyes. Take the time to notice and appreciate what you have. *Consider yourself fortunate.*

TIP # 86
Look on the bright side.

Think positive. Be optimistic. Don't be so hard on yourself. Smile! Things will get better. Sleep on it. Stop complaining. Tomorrow's another day. It won't hurt your eyes to look on the bright side.

Sometimes it's easier said than done. Perhaps you try but can't always find a bright side to see.

Would you like to feel better about yourself? Are you looking for success? It's on the bright side. Do you want health and happiness, peace of mind, and a new perspective? Just look on the bright side of things. Are you seeking more joy and less stress? You'll have it when you look on the bright side. Here's how to get started:

Change your view of the news. Whether you watch the news on TV, listen to the radio, read the paper, or view it online, it doesn't matter how you get the news as long as the news doesn't *get to you*.

News can be depressing; much of it generates stress and fear. You should know what's going on in the world, but you don't have to dwell on it. There's no need to listen to the same news reports several times a day.

If the news makes you anxious, don't watch the news at night; you might find you sleep better when you don't. Make a decision about how much news you want to hear and when you want to hear it. Seek positive news. There are good-news sites on the Internet, and you'll find some good-news programs on TV. Talk less about the bad news you hear and more about the good. You can change your view of the world by changing your view of the news.

Make sense out of senselessness. Some things make no sense: a six year-old brings a loaded gun to school, a drunk driver gets his fifth DWI, a newborn baby is found in a dumpster, and on it goes. You can shake your head in disbelief or look for the reasons why such things happen. Do people need to be more responsible? Do our laws protect us? What can be done to stop such sense-lessness? What would you like to see changed? It will help if you read *into* the news you hear rather than just read *about it*.

Do something. You may not be able to change the world, but you can change *something*. Don't sit back and complain about the problems you see; *do something*. Get involved; join an organiza-tion; write to your legislators, send a letter to your newspaper, or post your thoughts on an Internet bulletin board. Volunteer your time, donate needed goods, or send a financial contribution. Talk about what can be done. Educate those who do not know. It doesn't matter what you do as long as you *do something*, no matter how small—and it's better than doing nothing at all.

Look for the good in the bad. It's a fact of life; bad stuff happens. Life is *not* a bowl of cherries, and it's seldom fair. Both good and bad fortune is distributed randomly and inequitably. You can throw up your arms in despair or try to find some good in the bad. It's painful when a relationship or job comes to an end. However, endings often spur new beginnings; the things you learn from each experience often lead you to something else. The end of one relationship might result in a healthier, more loving relationship. The loss of a job often leads to a more challenging, better-paying job. Loss can lead to gain, pain can fuel compassion, and bad can turn into good.

Focusing on the good doesn't take away from the bad but can make it easier to bear. The good is not always apparent right away, but if you look, you'll find something positive.

Appreciate what you have. Have you ever wanted something so much it occupied your mind? Do you remember the excitement you felt when you finally got what you had been waiting for? How long did the good feeling last? Days, weeks, months, or years? We anticipate but too often fail to *appreciate* the things we have.

Do you appreciate what *you* have? Start with the basics; if you're able to move, see, speak, and hear, be thankful. Some people struggle every day to do the things you take for granted. Take time each day to think, write, or talk about the things you appreciate. The more grateful you are, the more you will find to be grateful for. Don't wait until it's too late; appreciate what you have while you have it.

Look on the bright side. Life is what you make it; you can look for, and see, the dark side of life or choose to look on the bright side of things. It's your life, and you can decide how dark or bright you want it to be. What you look for is what you'll see.

TIP # 87
Enjoy the ride.

Have you ever been on a roller coaster? Did you like it? Would you be willing to ride it again? Some people like the roller coaster. Others prefer the merry-go-round. Which do you prefer?

Some people fear the roller coaster. They focus on the problems and risks. Some people hold back; others let go. Some people scream, others weep, and some make no sound at all. Some people try to conquer their fears and decide to go for a ride. Others refuse. They sneer as they stand on the side and criticize those who try.

Some people prefer the merry-go-round because it moves slowly and provides a better view. It's a relaxing ride but not nearly as exciting as a roller coaster. You know what to expect on a merry-go-round; you know you keep going round and round.

Life is a lot like a roller coaster.

Life is unpredictable, with lots of twists and turns. At times it moves very slowly. At others it moves too fast.

Life is a thrilling adventure; you never know what will happen next. One minute you're up, and the next you're down. Life is filled with highs and lows.

Some people look forward in life; others look back. Some people look at everything, yet others see nothing at all. Some people focus on pleasure, but others concentrate on pain. Some people resist; others relax.

Life can seem brief or appear to last a very long time. No matter how thrilling, a good roller-coaster ride always comes to an end. The same is true in life. Strive to make sure you don't reach the end of your life until you've had *the ride of your life*.

TIP # 88

Life is *not* a game.

Some people think of life as a game. There are similarities between life and games; both can be played, both have rules, and both turn out winners and losers. Those who view life as a game might approach their lives methodically, living their lives the way they'd play a game of chess. Others might take more risks, gambling with life the way they gamble with money.

There are differences between the two, however. Games distract you from life; the more you play, the less you pay attention to the more important things in life. You can play a game as often as you want; you can play until you *win*.

In life, you get only one chance to *play*. *When your life is over, the game is over.*

Life is *not* a game. Life is the real thing. Life is unpredictable; you can play it right and still lose. Life is not always fair; one wrong move, one bad choice, is often one too many in life. Take a chance with your life and it could be the last chance you get.

Life isn't always fun, but it can be if you decide to make it that way. *Enjoy your life.* Take risks, but don't engage in *risky behavior*. Think about the things you do. Don't *play* with your life. You are young. You have a bright future. Protect your life.

Don't play with your safety. Don't ignore proven safety measures. Safety measures and safety gear have one purpose: to keep you *safe*. Wear your seat belt, wear a helmet, and wear knee and elbow pads. Wear a life jacket, wear sunscreen, and protect your eyes by wearing sunglasses. Wear a jacket, a scarf, hat, gloves, or mittens when it's cold. Your safety is in *your* hands; be safe.

Don't play with money. You can make your money grow or throw it all away. Don't pay with a credit card if you don't have the money to pay for the bill when it comes. No bargain is a bargain if you'll be paying interest on it for years to come. Save some of your money. Don't spend everything you have. Put some money aside for a rainy day. Think twice before making a purchase, no matter how small. Skip the candy bar, cup of coffee, or can of soda each day, and save the money you would have spent. In just a few years, you will have saved thousands of dollars. Save more, and you'll have more. The habits you develop today will affect you financially for the rest of your life. Learn how to manage your money.

Don't play with the law. Keep the law on *your* side. If you choose to break the law, you will pay the consequences, and you will have a record that will haunt you the rest of your life. Every time you apply for a job, you will be asked if you've ever been arrested or convicted of a crime. Do you see yourself as a criminal? Whether you do or don't, other people will. Take or sell illegal drugs and you are taking a big risk. Take something from someone and you are stealing, whether it's a small amount of money from someone's drawer or an item from a retail store. If you exceed the speed limit, cheat on your taxes, drink and drive, or break any other law, you are taking a huge risk. Laws are meant to protect you, and you can protect yourself by obeying the law.

Don't play with people's feelings. Be honest with yourself and others. If you are in a relationship you know is going nowhere, but the person you are with is looking for commitment, don't string him or her along. If you have a problem with someone, don't tell everyone else—tell that person. Treat others the way you'd like to be treated. Don't use people for what you hope to get. You'll get more when you give of yourself and treat people well. The more in touch you are with your own feelings, the easier it will be for you to feel for someone else.

Don't play with sex. Your body is not a toy, and sex is not a game. Don't say *yes* if you want to say *no*, and know that *no* means *no*. Don't confuse sex and love; if you want love, you won't get it by having sex. If you aren't comfortable talking with someone about your feelings or the decision to have sex with him or her, *don't*. If you think sex belongs in a committed relationship, be sure your partner thinks the same way. Anytime you decide to become sexually involved with someone, you put your life at risk. You can and should practice safe sex, but nothing (other than abstinence) provides you the assurance you need against pregnancy or disease. Sex is not a game. Don't play with sex; play it safe.

Don't play with your future. Think. Your future is at stake in everything you do. Do you envision owning a home, getting married, or having children? Do you want to start a business, run a marathon, or travel the world? Do you want to be healthy and maintain a youthful appearance? If there is something you want to do, start planning *now*. Every decision you make and everything you do will either help you accomplish your goals or make them more difficult to achieve. The future may seem far away, but your future is a result of what you do, starting today.

TIP # 89
Don't take rejection personally.

Rejection can be summed up in one word: OUCH! It *hurts* to be rejected, but it doesn't have to. Rejection can be good for you! As the saying goes, no pain, no gain. The struggles and setbacks in life will provide you with some of life's most valuable lessons.

Rejected? Put it in perspective.

- Rejection is a part of life. You can't always get what you want. Accept it and expect it to happen. When you are rejected, it isn't always about you.

- Rejection is inevitable. Consider it an aspect of your education. You can try out for the school play, the soccer team, choir, or any position you want. You will either make it or you won't. There usually are more people trying out than there are positions available. You or someone you know will experience rejection. It doesn't mean you are no good; it means other people fit the guidelines better.

● You can apply to as many colleges as you want, knowing you will reject those you choose not to attend and assuming some colleges will reject you. Most schools can accept only a certain number of new students each year. Why take it personally—thousands of others will be rejected too, so join the club!

● It takes courage to approach someone new. Salespeople do it all the time. Even the best salespeople hear "no" far more than they hear "yes," but they don't give up; every "no" they hear brings them closer to a "yes." It's a numbers game; why don't you play along?

● When you apply for a job, you set yourself up for rejection. If you aren't asked for an interview, it doesn't mean you are no good—it means there are more-qualified applicants than you. While your goal is to get your foot in the door, the goal of the person in charge of hiring is to find the best person for the job. Part of that job is rejecting a certain number of applicants. If you never get a call for an interview, don't blame yourself—blame your resume! If you interview for a position but don't get the job, it doesn't mean you did poorly; it means someone else did better!

● When someone wants to end a relationship with you, it doesn't mean you are unworthy, even if someone else tries to tell you so. Anyone who would say such a thing is the one who is unworthy. You may not want a relationship to end, but when it suddenly does, the relationship (or other person) probably wasn't as great as you thought. If someone hurt you in the end, think about the hurt you would have experienced if you had stayed.

If something you said or did makes someone so mad they won't talk to you, don't take it too personally. Just as you must control your anger, other people must control theirs. Most anger is misdirected anyway. The person may be upset with him or herself or someone else but decided to take it out on you. Welcome this type of rejection—you don't need people like this in your life.

 When someone is harsh with you, judgmental, or critical, don't assume you are wrong. A person who finds fault with everyone else generally is unhappy with him or herself.

Rejection is seldom a personal affront. Learn what you can from each experience; then move on. The way you feel about what happened will change over time. You will see things differently in the future. Every successful person has been rejected—and more than once.

TIP # 90
Respond; don't overreact.

Life is full of surprises. No matter how prepared you think you are, you never know what each new day will bring. It has been said that whatever happens *to you* in life is less important than *how you respond* to what happens. You may not be able to control everything that happens, but you *can* choose your response to the things that happen to you.

If someone accused you of something you didn't do, how would you respond? Would you take time to *think* about your response or allow your emotions to take over and react without thinking? When you're upset, do you tend to talk quickly or slowly, loudly or quietly? Do you yell and pound your fist or become tongue-tied and shut down?

If you were a patient in an emergency room, would you prefer a doctor who responded calmly or reacted emotionally? How would you feel if the doctor who was to care for you began screaming hysterically, swearing, or yelling? Doctors are always expecting the unexpected. An emotional reaction won't help anyone under such circumstances. When you are a patient, your life depends on a doctor's ability to respond calmly and effectively.

Most emotional reactions and overreactions are due to an element of surprise. No one *expects* an accident. You don't *plan* to lose your job, miss a meeting, or lose a valuable item. An emotional reaction to such events is not unusual, but the question is whether or not it is *helpful*.

Losing your temper or your composure when your flight is delayed, when you're stuck in traffic, have misplaced your keys, or are dissatisfied with the service you receive is neither appropriate nor acceptable. In contrast to other things in life, such inconveniences are hardly worth becoming agitated over, yet these types of incidents provoke emotional reactions all the time.

You might try to respond calmly, but trying isn't the same as *doing*. Saying "I'll try" is like saying "I might" or "I'm not sure I can." Do you *try* to go to work or do you go to work? Do you *try* to exercise, or do you get up and move? Do you *try* to remember a friend's birthday, or do you remember it? You either do something or you don't.

You can *choose* your response the same way you *choose* the clothes you wear, the food you eat, the TV show you watch, and the words you use.

If you tend to overreact, think about more effective ways to respond. Don't wait until the next time you feel your emotions taking over; identify what *isn't* working and what kind of response will work better instead.

Sometimes the best response to a person or situation is *no response*. If you aren't comfortable responding at the time, saying "I need some time to think" or "I'm not sure how to respond to your comment" is preferable to saying something you'll later regret. When you take time to think things through, you are *responding*, not *reacting*, to what happens. You will have fewer regrets, make better decisions, and exercise self-control.

TIP # 91
Learn to laugh at yourself.

When was the last time you had a really good laugh? Not just a little chuckle, but a *hearty* laugh? When was the last time you laughed so hard you had to stop to catch your breath or had tears running down your face? If you can't remember, it's been too long.

Laughter is *good* for you. In addition to the aerobic benefits you gain from laughing, laughter can reduce stress, lower blood pressure, and ease pain.

If you want to laugh but have nothing to laugh about, don't despair; what's funny to one person isn't always funny to another. Identify your own brand of humor, and if you look, you will find things to laugh about.

You don't have to be funny or have a lot of funny things happen in your life; just look for the funny things that happen each day. Learn from comedians, who know how to turn a common occurrence into a hilarious event. Comedians aren't afraid to look silly; they thrive on their humiliation. An embarrassing moment often is the basis of a hilarious story to tell. Some of your best laughs will be the result of your most embarrassing moments *if* you are willing to see the humor in what happens instead of the humiliation.

Not long ago, I slipped and fell in the detergent aisle of the grocery store. It happened so fast I wasn't sure how I ended up on the floor. My daughter was at the other end of the aisle and I expected her to help me, but instead she was walking the other way. She wanted nothing to do with me. I felt rather sorry for myself and was about to get mad, but when I saw her laughing uncontrollably, I wanted to know what she thought was so funny. As she told me what she had witnessed, I started laughing too. The more we embellished and talked about the details, the funnier it became. For the rest of the shopping trip, we couldn't look at each other without laughing. My stomach muscles were sore, not from falling but from laughing so hard.

Learn to laugh at life; learn to laugh at yourself.

Lighten up! Don't get too worked up about the little things in life. Will the thing you're stressed about today be remembered a year from now? Will it matter five years from today? Don't hang on to perfection or stress; learn to *let go* of the things you can't control.

Accentuate the funny side of life. You'll find humor almost anywhere if you look for it. Do you ever watch late-night television? David Letterman is known for his top-ten lists; Jay Leno for his headline segments. These segments bring out the humorous, unusual side of the day's events. Don't overlook the more unusual side of life; accentuate the funny side of things.

Use humor. A little humor can go a long way. Observe comedians and other people you think are funny. Listen to the way they talk about themselves and about life. If you heard a joke that made you laugh, write it down and read it again—consider sharing it with someone. You don't have to be armed with jokes or try to entertain your friends, but be willing to laugh with others, and don't be afraid to laugh at yourself.

Get up and go out. Get up and go out to a comedy club, a funny movie, or a play. Go to a bookstore, a coffee shop, or to visit a friend. Go roller skating, bowling, or anywhere you haven't been. If you feel like a fool doing something you haven't done before, it can be fun *and* funny.

Have more fun! All work and no play will hurt anyone's funny bone. Make sure you make time for fun times. Play fun games, tell funny stories, and do something fun for yourself. The more fun you have, the more likely you will find something to laugh about.

The next time you're feeling ill or a little blue, laugh and see what it does for you. Laughter really is the best medicine. Laugh yourself to good health.

TIP # 92

Change is inevitable; misery is optional.

When Ann Ulrich's husband came home from work with "that look" on his face, she knew what it meant; he had been fired. She knew she had to do *something*. She decided to throw a party to celebrate her husband's job loss. Her husband was less enthusiastic about the idea, but once he redirected his anger and frustration over his job loss into planning his celebration, his perspective changed. As they planned the details of his job-loss celebration, they both grew increasingly optimistic about the turn of events and the possibilities the future held.

The original "I Got Fired! Party" was a success. Not only did her husband benefit, but she did too. As a result of her experience, she founded Celebrate Transitions, Inc. and created the IGotFiredParty.com website. She is dedicated to helping others learn how to celebrate their job loss too.

Job loss is not something typically celebrated. There is no right or wrong response to being fired. Everyone reacts differently, but few react joyfully. Losing a job is rarely considered good news. But it forces you to take a good look at your life and yourself, whether you want to or not. Throwing a party is both a positive and proactive response to job loss. It is easier than calling everyone you know and telling the same story repeatedly and a great way to network and let others know you are looking for work.

Change isn't easy; anything you can do to minimize the stress you feel is beneficial. There are many uncertainties in life, but change is constant.

You are evolving and changing too. Just look through an old photo album to see how much you have *changed*. You've changed physically since the day you were born, and you will continue to do so. You're knowledge changes, and so does your perspective. Your experiences, both good and bad, have shaped your view of the world and are part of you.

You can *resist* change or you can accept and embrace it. You can make it easier or more difficult. Either way, change will occur. It is inevitable. If you resist change, what are you resisting? Are you:

Denying the truth?

Trying to control things you have no control over?

Saying no to new opportunities?

Opposed to different or better ways of doing things?

Resisting new knowledge?

Limiting your potential?

Change is inevitable, and it can be *positive*.

- Change can help you face and conquer your fears.
- Change can lead to better relationships, a better job, and a better life.
- Change can teach you something new.
- Change can produce compassion.
- Change can broaden your perspective.
- Change can motivate you to take action.
- Change can be good; focus on the positive aspects of change.

You don't have to *like* change to *accept* it; you can learn to cope with change. Only you can choose whether you will resist or accept it. *Celebrate* the changes that occur in your life.

TIP # 93
Sometimes you have to let go.

Some things are worth fighting for, but others are better off left alone. You should fight for what you believe and work hard for the things you want. Hold on to your dreams, your values, and your self-respect. Hold on to those you love. Hold on, but don't hang on; know when it's time to let go.

Letting go isn't easy, but neither is hanging on. When you let go, you give up control. Giving up is *not* the same as giving in. When you give something up, you release it; you free yourself of your need for control. Trying to control what you cannot is a daunting task. The longer you hang on to something, the more you hurt yourself. You deplete your physical and emotional energy when you try to have power over anything that is out of your hands.

- **Let go of your fear.** If you're hanging on because you are *afraid* of letting go, let go of your fear; you've nothing to be afraid of.

- **Let go of your need to be right.** If you're hanging on because you don't want to be wrong, let go of your need to be right.

- **Let go of your need to control other people.** If you're hanging on to a relationship because you don't want to lose someone, it's likely you've already lost him or her. You can't make someone love you, want to be with you, or be the kind of person *you* want him or her to be.

- **Let go of your grudges.** When you hold a grudge, you hold on to your anger and you hold yourself back. Don't allow your anger to get the best of you. The person you forgive isn't the only one who gets a break—you will feel better too.

- **Let go of your need for perfection.** No one is perfect and neither are you. What's the point in setting standards too impossible to meet? Set your standards high, but make sure they are within reach.

- **Let go of guilt.** No one can *make* you feel guilty. Anyone can try, but guilt is something you bring on yourself.

● **Let go of your judgments.** You are not superior and have no right to criticize or pass judgment on others. Look inward instead of outward. The more you look for and find fault with others, the more likely you are to see that similar weakness within yourself. Focus on what you can control; focus on you.

● **Let go of worry.** Worry does nothing but cause more worry. No amount of worry will prevent something from happening or help you deal with it if it does. Worry is a waste of time. You can't predict the future. Life is unpredictable. Stop worrying, stop predicting, and start enjoying life and living.

You can let go and still hang on to your hopes and dreams. You can let go and still fight for what you believe. If you can't change it, resolve it, or control it, do the one thing you can do: Let it go.

TIP # 94
Put on a happy face.

You've heard many messages about the impact of your attitude and the importance of maintaining a positive attitude. It isn't difficult to understand that a cheerful disposition is preferable and that optimism is something to strive for. If you want to make yourself and others feel better, look pleasant, and be happier, just put on a happy face.

You've probably heard it or even suggested it yourself: "Snap out of it." "Don't worry." "Be happy." "*Look* happy." If someone suggested these things when you didn't feel like snapping out of it or smiling, the encouragement to do so may have made matters worse. When you are feeling down, being told to cheer up will not necessarily make you feel any better, but the truth is it could.

A positive attitude will help you in many ways. When you have a good outlook, and it shows, you will find it easier to meet people and make new friends, increase your chances of career success, improve your relationships, and make everything you do more enjoyable.

Thinking positively is *good* for you in other ways too. Studies have found a correlation between mental health and physical health. Positive people tend to be healthier than their negative counterparts. An optimistic outlook is good for the immune system; the more positive you are, the stronger your immune system is likely to be and the better able you are to fight off illness and disease.

Happy, emotionally healthy individuals *live longer* than those who are unhappy, negative, and pessimistic about their future. One of the simplest ways to change your attitude is by *smiling*. *Smile* and your eyes sparkle; *smile* and you appear friendly; *smile* and you soften the lines in your face; *smile* and you look happier; *smile* and you *feel* happier too.

Don't underestimate the value of the expression on your face. Think about the times you've looked at someone and could tell he or she was mad or sad. We speak with our faces although we may never say a word. It's easy to tell when someone shouldn't be disturbed; we understand the silent language when someone's face says "leave me alone."

If you aren't meeting the right kind of people or finding the job you want, the reason could be as simple as the expression on your face. Not sure? Look around you and notice the people you see. How many *look* happy? Compare those who look happy with those who don't. Which are you attracted to?

Work on improving your attitude. Look on the bright side. You don't have to feel happy to look happy. Sometimes looking happy can help you to feel that way. Don't try to solve all of your problems; just start by doing one thing differently. Changing the expression on your face may seem too simple to do any good, but try it and see for yourself what a difference it can make. Your expression can literally change your life. Even if you have nothing to smile about, smile anyway. The more you smile, the better you will feel; your life will begin to change for the better. People will smile back. Some people may even speak to you. You've got nothing to lose. If you want to improve your attitude and live a long, healthy life, you have to start somewhere. Why not start with your face?

TIP # 95
Learn to give and receive compliments.

I hardly recognized Sherry when I ran into her unexpectedly at the mall. I hadn't seen her in some time but had talked with her on the phone about the operation she had to help her lose weight. "You look wonderful," I said. I was about to be more specific, but she interrupted me. She rolled her eyes and said "Wonderful? Are you kidding? Look at me. I'm a mess! My shirt is stained, my hair is greasy, and my clothes are practically falling off of me. You need to get your eyes checked."

I was dumbfounded. Sherry had lost a substantial amount of weight since the last time I saw her. She *did* look good. I wasn't scrutinizing her, and I wouldn't have noticed any of the imperfections she was determined to draw my attention to.   Instead of focusing on the positive outcome of her weight loss, she focused only on the negative, pointing out all of her perceived flaws.

Sherry not only made herself look bad, but she made me look pretty bad too. Rather than listening to and accepting my compliment, she *criticized* me for giving it. As if that weren't enough, she contradicted everything I said.

Sherry isn't the only one who has trouble accepting a compliment. Most of us want reassurance and praise, yet when we actually get it, we don't know what to do with it. When we feel insecure or undeserving of the praise we receive, we tend to refute it.

Think about your reaction to the compliments you receive. Do you graciously accept other people's comments? Consider a compliment as a gift. When someone gives you a gift, he or she hopes you will appreciate and accept it. Imagine how you would feel if you gave someone a gift, but instead of graciously accepting it, the person gave it back to you. When you receive a compliment, it might make *you* feel more comfortable to reject it, but think about the impact on the person who gave it to you. That person might feel uncomfortable when you do.

Accept the compliments you receive, and be generous in giving compliments to others. Do you look for, and talk freely about, the positive things people do? Or do you feel threatened, afraid that doing so will make someone else look better than *you?*

When you make someone else look good, you make yourself look good too. Look for the good in others, and then tell people what you see. Be careful you don't use flattery; a genuine compliment comes from *within*.

Make it easy for others to receive your compliments; be sincere, specific, and succinct. And make it easy for others who compliment you; don't debate or negate a compliment. Accept and appreciate it. A simple "thank you" is all you need to say.

Be a generous giver and a gracious receiver; learn to give and receive compliments and see for yourself how rewarding both can be.

TIP # 96
Be a cheerleader for yourself and others.

You don't have to be a big fan of baseball to know about the World Series or a die-hard football fan to be familiar with the Super Bowl. These are two of the biggest sporting events held each year. These offer a time when people gather together to watch and cheer, and do you know why? Because it's more fun than watching, cheering, or celebrating alone.

Would a game be as exciting to watch, or as thrilling for the players to play, if there were no fans cheering them on? Professional athletes rely on their fans to cheer them on. but they aren't the only ones; *everyone* does better with a little encouragement. You don't have to play a professional sport to surround yourself with fans.

Who surrounds *you?* Are your friends and family on your "team"? Do they want you to win? Will they celebrate your success? Do you hear more cheering or more jeering? Are you a cheerleader for others? Can you feel happy (not envious) for another person's success?

You're fortunate if you have people cheering for you, but the most important cheerleader in your life is *you*. You need to be your biggest fan. You have to rely on yourself. Only *you* can motivate you. It's important to have support from others, but ultimately, your motivation comes from *you*.

Listen to yourself. Do you speak highly of yourself and others? Do you criticize more than you praise? Are you more inclined to say "good job" or "you could have done better," "I'm doing okay" or "I'm feeling great," "I told you so" or "at least you tried"? Listen to the things you say; if your words aren't supportive, *you* aren't supportive.

Be a good sport. Are you happy for the successes of others, or do you compare someone else's success to your own? Is your attitude consistent, or are you a fair-weather fan? When times are tough, do you give up on yourself and others or keep cheering on? We all need a boost when the going gets tough, and we need encouragement to go on. Be a cheerleader *all* of the time; be consistent.

Cheer for yourself. You won't feel like a winner if you call yourself a loser, and you'll find it difficult to accomplish much if you tell yourself you can't. Tell yourself the things you need to hear repeatedly. The more you cheer, the easier it will be to believe in what you hear yourself saying.

Cheer for others. Do you find fault with others or look for what's right? Do you point out problems or look for solutions? Do you hold people back or push people forward? Are you inclined to say "keep it up" or "give it up," "you're doing the best you can," or "you could have done better?" The more you cheer for others, the more they will cheer for you.

Celebrate your triumphs. Remind yourself of your success by creating your own hall of fame. Proudly display the awards, ribbons, and certificates you receive. Save the nice notes and cards you get so you can read them when you need a cheer to get you going. Display pictures of happy and special moments in your life, and look at them often or anytime you need a boost. You don't need to win the World Series to feel you've accomplished something big. Celebrate the little things and the big things and cheer yourself on.

Learn a new cheer. If you don't know how to cheer, you can learn. A cheer must be sincere; make sure you *sound* excited. Start slowly; work on a new cheer each week. Practice saying the cheer until you feel you've got it right. Here are a few cheers to get you started:

Way to go!

You did it!

WOW!

You're really coming along!

Congratulations!

Good job!

You outdid yourself!

This is fantastic!

Right on!

You've learned fast!

That's great!

You're almost there!

I'm so proud of you!

Areas of Distinction

Rise Above the Ordinary and Live an Extraordinary Life

TIP # 97

Volunteer.

It's important to live intentionally. You need to know who you are and where you are going. The more focused you are, the better off you are. The busier you are, the more productive you are. Ironically, it's the people who are the busiest that we rely on the most to get things done. But time is precious, and you may find more things you'd like to do than you have time to do them.

You might be inclined to say no when you are asked to volunteer, but think twice before you respond negatively. Volunteering is always optional, but it can be very worthwhile and it's something you should consider carving out the time to do. When you share some of your talent and success or some of what you have with others, you will enjoy and appreciate it more. There will always be people with more and people with less than you. Pay attention to both, but pay special attention to those who can use your help.

You don't have to make a big commitment to volunteer. In fact, you need to be careful not to over-commit. If you try to do too much, you won't help anyone. Be selective and carefully choose the volunteer opportunities that appeal most to you. Then get involved and commit only to those things you can see through to completion.

You don't get paid money when you volunteer, but what you get is something money can't buy. You get the personal satisfaction that comes from doing something good, and you may get experience otherwise unavailable to you. When you volunteer and improve life for others, your life will change for the better because it will improve too.

Look for volunteer opportunities through work and outside of work. If you don't know what kind of opportunity you want, there are volunteer organizations that can use your help and help you figure out what you're most suited to do.

- Volunteer one day or evening a week, once a month, or a few times a year; it doesn't really matter as long as you find time to volunteer.

- Volunteer to donate money, food, clothing, or whatever an organization needs. Or, instead of buying and sending cards on a special occasion, send a card from the recipient's favorite charity informing them you've made a donation.

- Volunteer your home; house a foreign exchange student, or offer to hold a meeting or event at your home. Become a foster parent; there are many children needing temporary shelter and there are just as many abandoned pets.

- Volunteer your expertise. Charities and organizations need different types of expertise. Share your knowledge with others and help out an organization or person in need.

- Volunteer and do something you are passionate about. You're bound to learn something new and meet other passionate people who share your interests too.

- Volunteer to mentor others. Become a big brother or sister. Give encouragement; be someone's life coach. Get involved in a mentoring program.

- Volunteer to help out a friend or neighbor; volunteer to help the sick, the elderly, or anyone unable to care for him or herself.

- Volunteer selflessly; volunteer because you want to give, not because there's something you're hoping to get. Volunteer because you want to do something for someone else, but don't be surprised when you benefit from volunteering yourself.

TIP # 98
Make a difference.

Lois was only 52 when she died. People came from near and far to honor her memory and celebrate her life. Anyone in attendance wanting to pay tribute to her was encouraged to speak up, and people of all ages, from every walk of life, stepped forward to share their stories.

Rebecca, the first to speak, both laughed and cried as she talked about her best friend. "Lois thought I was so funny, she wanted to hire someone to follow me around to write down everything I said. I'm here to tell you that I'm not the one worth writing about—Lois is. She had a way of making me feel so special; she made *everyone* feel special."

Everyone who got up to speak told similar stories. Lois wasn't famous or featured in the headlines, but she had a profound impact on those who knew her. She made a positive difference in people's lives.

Lois accomplished what many do not; she lived a happy and meaningful life. In his book *When All You've Ever Wanted Isn't Enough*, Harold Kushner says people do not fear death as much as they fear leaving a life that had no meaning. What people fear most is the thought that their life hasn't mattered—no one wants to be forgotten. The happiest people, he says, aren't those who *pursue* happiness but those who, by being good people, live meaningful lives.

Some people are deeply connected to the importance and purpose of their lives, while others are not. Everyone finds meaning in different ways. Some people seek significance through their work and accomplishments; others rely on their relationships or the deeds they perform. How do you find meaning in your life? What do you hope to accomplish during your lifetime? What's the most important thing you want to do? What kind of person do you want to be?

Who are the most important people in your life? How do you want to be remembered by them when you are gone? In what ways would you like the world to be different because of *you*?

You might think what you do doesn't matter, but it does. You might think one person can't make a difference, but one person can and often does. Think about the individuals who have influenced *your* life. Then ask yourself if they know who they are. If you haven't done so yet, be sure to tell them the difference they've made. When you do, you'll be making a difference in their lives too.

You're on this earth for a reason, and it's not to take up space. No one can tell you what you are meant to do, but there is a reason. Search for your purpose.

As you begin to build your life, the end may seem far away. You want to think about living, not dying, but you should think about the legacy you want to leave behind some day. Start thinking about it *now* and start making a difference today.

TIP # 99
Cross the finish line.

No matter how many projects you start, your achievements are a result of what you *finish*. It doesn't matter what you think about doing or plan to do; you get credit only for what you *complete*.

People don't *plan* on stopping a project in the middle or as they near the end, but all too often they do. Some say it's because of a fear of failure; others say it's a fear of success. The best antidote for fear is to face and conquer it.

You won't end up where you want by quitting. The only way you win is when you *cross the finish line.*

How many books have been bought but never read? How many photo albums have sit empty with no pictures because we're too busy to fill them? How many songs have been written but never sung? How many manuscripts are being written but won't ever be finished?

Why do we make promises we cannot keep? Why do we start things we never complete? What gets in the way? What gets in *your* way?

Do you quit when you think you cannot win? If so, stop thinking about winning and start thinking about *doing.* Did you know that *winners never quit?* Those who quit will never win.

Do you say yes when you want to say no? If so, how will you motivate yourself to see the project through? Remember, you can't please everyone. Say yes only to the things that are most important to you.

Do you have things you know you'll regret if you don't get them done? If so, put these tasks at the top of your list and make it a priority to finish them. You may never get another chance to tell someone how you feel—or to visit someone who is terminally ill. If you wait too long, you might be too late to do anything at all.

Do you have a list of things you don't want to do but feel you *ought* to? If so, determine how important it is. If it's important, you should do it. Exercise is important, and we all ought to exercise, but we don't because it's easy to procrastinate. If you wait to exercise until your life depends on it, it could be too late.

Do you have things you plan on finishing *someday*? If so, decide *when* that someday will be. The someday you're waiting for may never come unless you assign a deadline to it.

Do you have things you plan on doing when you find the time? If so, you need to realize you will never *find* time. You have to *make* time to do the things you want to do. If you haven't found more time by now, chances are you never will.

Do you have things you'd like to do that aren't important? If so, cross them off your list and put them out of your mind. Focus on doing only the most important things.

Do you have things you want to do but aren't sure you can? If so, you can do anything you set your mind to. Find the strength to see it through, and consider asking someone to help you.

Do you have trouble finishing things because you're never satisfied? If so, focus on *doing* your best, and stop worrying about *being* the best. You'll never get much done if you're striving for perfection.

You don't get credit for the things you *think* about doing or *plan* to do someday. You get credit only for what you *do* each day.

Make a list of all the things you want to do; then decide which tasks are most important to you. Focus on the most important ones and make a plan to get them done. It's easier to finish when you carefully consider what you start.

Be a *doer*, not a quitter. You let yourself down when you stop short of a goal, but you will feel like a winner every time you **cross the finish line.**

TIP # 100
Believe.

This is *your* life. Decide how you want your life to be. You can either stay where you are or set yourself free to become the person you know you can be. You can accomplish anything you want as long as you *believe.*

Some people believe they are destined to fail; others believe they will succeed. What you believe has *everything* to do with what you achieve. It doesn't matter what others believe you can or cannot do. What matters is what *you* believe you can do.

Martin Luther King Jr. *believed.* He had a dream *and* the courage to share it with others.

Helen Keller could not hear or see, but she managed to have a *vision*; she accomplished more than most, despite the number of obstacles she faced.

Marilyn Monroe, Elvis Presley, and the Beatles were all told they wouldn't succeed, but they *did*. They didn't believe what others predicted their fate would be.

No one else knows what's best for you. Only you know what you believe. Look for the motive when someone tells you what you should or shouldn't do. Is this person thinking about what's best for you? Anyone who discourages you might be discouraged himself. Perhaps he (or she) once had a dream and let it slip away. It's not easy supporting someone else's dream if you've given up on your own.

It hurts to stop believing. When you give up on yourself, all you're left with are thoughts of what *might* have been.

Life is full of choices. Decide *now* how you want your life to be. You can't be wrong about a decision if it's right for *you*.

Have a vision—picture the way you want your life to be. Believe in your vision. Believe you will rise each time you fall. Believe you are meant to reach your dreams. *Believe*.

TIP # 101
Never give up on your dreams.

I was working on writing my final few tips when my daughter, Stephanie, and I were talking about my dreams for this book. She asked me *why* I decided to write the book. There were and are so many reasons that I had trouble giving her a simple answer. Writing this book was something I wanted to do, but even more, it was something I was *compelled* to do.

When I came up with the idea for this book, I assumed it would be similar to other projects I've done. It wasn't. Because this is a book about *life,* with each tip I wrote, I looked closely at how I was living it in my own life. I couldn't write authentically about something I hadn't dealt with or didn't know about, so in the process of writing I discovered work I had to do. As I encouraged you to grow and change, I was growing and changing too.

If anyone had told me when I was younger about the things I'd be doing today, I wouldn't have believed a word. In fact, no one else would have believed it either. I wasn't a failure, but I wasn't much of a success either. I can't say I've struggled as much as some people, but I've had my share of challenges and obstacles and have learned many of life's lessons the *hard* way.

It's one of the many reasons I wrote this book. I don't want you to struggle more than you have to. I want you to understand what's expected of you, what works, and what doesn't. I want you to make the most of yourself and your life. Most of all, I want you to believe in your dreams—to know that anything is possible. It doesn't matter who you've been. Your future success is a result of who you become.

People frequently assume I'm a journalist or communications major, but I am not. I wasn't a star student in any classroom, and I didn't graduate from a prestigious university. However, I'm sure I would have received all A's if I'd been graded on what I learned as a student of *life*. I've always been a dreamer and determined to excel despite the adversity I faced.

I know you've heard it before, but have you ever really thought about what it means to *never give up on your dreams?*

It takes courage to dream. It's lonely when you have to defend something only you can see. It's not easy when people question your motives or discourage you. It takes strength to hold on to a dream you fear is slipping away. *Will you hold on to your dreams?* More than anything, I hope you do.

You have everything going for you. You've just completed the first few chapters of your life. Part of your story is written; the rest is yet to be told. *You* are the author and you've got empty pages to fill. Only you can determine the details of the story that will eventually be a reflection of the way you've lived your life.

Writing a book isn't easy. Some people have a tough time getting started; others struggle when they reach the end. It's not easy facing yourself. You won't always like what you see, but through the experience you will learn and grow. When you reach the final chapter you will see how close you came to fulfilling your dreams. You can either wait or decide now what you want your outcome to be.

The *only* reason I've accomplished anything, including writing the final words in this book, is because I *dared to dream* and *never quit.*

There are 101 tips in this book, and there is valuable information in each and every one.

The message I leave you with, however, is most crucial and is what I wish most for you:

Never **give up on your dreams.**

Appendix

Extra Credit Bonus Insights

I had no idea what I would find when I began my research for this book. I had plenty of my own advice to offer new graduates, and I had a feeling others had just as much to say. I wanted to provide the right mix of advice and didn't want to miss anything important. There's so much I wish I had known earlier in my life and I was sure there were others who felt the same. They did, and they responded to my request. I asked a selection of people working in a variety of industries the following questions:

What advice would you give to a recent graduate about to enter the 'real' world?

What is the best advice you ever received and how did it affect you?

What's the most important lesson you've learned since your graduation?

If you had it to do all over again, what would you do differently?

Many people selflessly offered to share their personal stories, words of wisdom, and hard-learned insights. The majority of responses came through e-mail, although I did conduct a number of interviews over the phone. Some people offered their comments and asked for no attribution, preferring to remain anonymous. Others requested only their names be used. Still others included their names, titles, and company information, and each quote that follows has been attributed according to the wishes of the person who gave it. All, however, contributed because they want to help you, the new graduate, get a jumpstart on your personal and professional success.

Experience really is the best teacher, and you will learn the most from your own personal experiences. No matter how many times you hear something, it will always have more impact when you can relate first hand to the information you receive. However, the more knowledge you have and the more aware you are, the better able you will be to make good decisions and deal with whatever you face. These insights can help prepare you for what's ahead and help guide you as you grow and make important decisions about your future.

This extra section is filled with bonus tips for you. You get "extra credit" for reading them, but the real credit goes to each and every person who took the time to respond. These insights represent the various responses I received and although I wish I could have included all of them in their entirety, I wish I could have included all the various responses I received, but I am sure you will find value in what is here. For easy referencing, these insights have been broken down into the same categories as the other tips in this book. I am sure you will enjoy reading what others have to say and will benefit from their experience and I trust you'll refer to this insight often.

WORK SKILLS

Find a job in a company that you are passionate about. Take any job necessary to get your foot in the door and be prepared to prove yourself over and over again until they can't help but notice your pure and total genius. Make yourself indispensable. Do not expect them to see said genius until you have consistently exhibited it over and over again. Work really hard. But don't forget to stay well rounded outside of the job as well. If you get lost in the job, you will lose yourself when you lose that job.

Carrie Heckman,
Vice President of Marketing,
Civilian Pictures

Growing up we all hear, "Just do your best." Well, one of the hardest lessons for me to learn was that sometimes your best is not good enough....Sometimes you will lose the game, the client, or the account. At times like these, I look at the process. Did I do everything I could to achieve the outcome I wanted? If you did everything you could...that is your best. You may not be a winner, but you win because you gave it your best.

Susan Edwards, M.S.
3D Productivity Consulting

Making mistakes is one of the critical ways that people learn. It is okay to make mistakes; however, it is important to keep making new mistakes. When you make a mistake, it gets you curious about how to fix it. Don't spend time trying to find the source of whom or what to blame; figure out what you can do to prevent the mistake from happening next time and move on.

Robbin Walker

Think of each job you have in your career as a learning and growing experience. The first few may not be the "job of your dreams" but work hard, focus, and keep a positive attitude. Do this and you'll develop yourself into a valuable resource, and people will notice. Never quit without another job lined up. Eventually you'll be the executive admiring a recent graduate with the same dedicated work ethic!

Alexander M. Costakis,
Managing Director,
Hollywood Stock Exchange, LLC

As hard as it may seem, doing a good job for your employer because it is the right thing to do makes all the difference in job satisfaction. Can you imagine the uncommon reactions from bosses and coworkers when you respond to criticism and even unfair treatment when you are motivated by doing the right thing. I strongly advise...be on time, stay a little later than most, and if you promise a deliverable, then [meet the] deadline.

Steve Hall, C.P.C.,
Senior Consultant, FGP International

It is important to remember that it takes time to prove yourself to a company. Have some patience. Go above and beyond what is expected and learn from everything you can and your opportunities for getting ahead will come.

Let someone know what you want—a boss, another manager, someone you can trust. It's hard to get what you want if no one knows you want it.

Be flexible, be open to new opportunities, take some chances, and you'll have an interesting and rewarding life. Many people will never know the "right answer" to the question, "What do I want to be?" but they can have a fun ride trying to figure it out.

Anonymous

I have learned that it is really important to have some expertise, knowledge, or skill in one thing versus a little bit of knowledge in many things.

Robin Stein

Whatever you do, love it. No matter how small the task, put your all into it. When I care about what I'm doing, I not only enjoy my work more, but I take more from it—skills, insight, etc.—that I can apply to bigger jobs in the future.

Laurie Katz,
Director of Publicity, Facts On File, Inc.

One of the things I learned about being in the career services industry is that a recent grad's first job sets the pace for his or her entire career. This is why it is important for them to not take the first offer that comes along.

Linda Matias,
President, CareerStrides and the
National Resume Writers' Association

One way or another, as pressured as I felt at the moment, as overwhelming as it all seemed, it all gets done. Once I truly embraced that concept, I was healthier in my outlook, relaxed more, and was more balanced. I still work very hard. But now I know to trust that it all gets done.

Maggie Mortenson

Don't enter any job thinking your diploma will get you through because it will not. The diploma only opens the door, but you still must prove yourself. I would tell any young person entering the business world "you must earn the respect and confidence of your coworkers and superiors."

Anonymous

Over the years I've worked in both large corporate settings and small businesses, in all sectors—private, nonprofit, and profit. The most important things I wish I'd known when I graduated are: (1) to do even the smallest and most menial tasks cheerfully and well, and (2) to realize that my job was to make my boss look good. It all starts with doing the small stuff.

Anonymous

One of the first things for a graduate to realize is that your first job may help determine the direction of your career, but it is not the only determinant. This means that one has to consider a given job at hand from many different perspectives [other] than just the immediate role or job definition. [Such as] what skills does it [the job] use and what skills may it help develop?

Shefaly Yogendra,
Technology Policy and Strategy Consultant

Your degree is an accomplishment. It doesn't entitle you to anything. The effort you put forth and the attitude that you approach your work and others with can either help you or hurt you...as you enter the work world.

LaChel Hird
LarsonAllen

While employee benefits are important considerations, ask a perspective employer about their corporate culture. If they value their employees as one of their best assets you may be on the path toward a rewarding and fulfilling career.

Sandra D. Bullock,
Vice President Institutional Sales,
Wells Fargo Brokerage Services, LLC

Be cognizant of the environment that you choose to work in. Toxic work life can infect, negatively, all areas of your life. Realize that you do have choices and yet, that doesn't mean you won't have to work hard. Keep your options open.

Peggy L. McNamara,
author of *My Tender Soul – A Story of Survival*

Find a mentor and maximize the relationship. Focus on what will make you successful in the company culture and key things you can do to stand out.

Danielle Devine
Vice President, Public Relations,
Johnson & Johnson Personal Products Company

COMMUNICATION SKILLS

Be trustworthy. Don't get involved in the gossip mill. Keep confidences. Keep your word.

Anonymous

Admit mistakes as soon as possible. These can impact company monies and your professional reputation, so it is wise to address these quickly to prevent bigger issues. An employee who readily admits he made the mistake earns more respect than the employee who doesn't own up to the error.

Anonymous

Be a sponge—listening is critical. Don't feel compelled to comment on everything; it's okay to be in [a] learning mode.

Danielle Devine
Vice President, Public Relations,
Johnson & Johnson Personal Products Company

Never lie. None of us has a good enough memory to remember everything we've ever said to everyone. Conversely, almost everyone possesses a gift for remembering everything anyone ever said to them. If you're caught in a lie, your credibility is damaged for a long time, if not forever. That's too high a price to pay. Tell the truth or remain silent, but never, never lie.

Sharron Stockhausen
CEO, Expert Publishing, Inc.

My mother once told me that "Confidence is a double-edged sword. Possessing too much or too little can be disastrous. Use it wisely and you will get ahead."

An individual's confidence level says much about the person, and nowhere is it more scrutinized than in a job interview. Job interviews are usually a one-shot chance to get the door opened further. A candidate is judged from the minute they enter the room. Character assessments are subjective and are made from a person's carriage, posture, and diction. Too little confidence is offensive and can be construed as someone who thinks they know-it-all. Success is reached when the candidate has the ability to discern the degree of confidence the interviewer is looking for and give them what they want. In other words, a successful candidate doesn't...sweat and knows when to keep his/her mouth shut.

Anonymous

Practice communicating! Take informal courses on interviewing techniques; learn to clearly articulate ideas, with concise and brief answers; get to the point; do not go off on tangents; utilize examples in your discussions; discuss how you can help the other (company, or person, or business, etc.)

Be prepared! Separate yourself from the rest of the crowd by being ready, well prepared, punctual, and do one thing different, better, and more special than the others. Leave something behind, make an impression, insure they remember you, insure they talk about you, stay focused, and be patient.

Henry Stein

Listen to friends; sometimes they see you better than you see yourself. I only hope that young people starting out have a good support system and can communicate with people that they trust to help them find what it is that they really want to do with their lives.

Anonymous

Always seek to improve your communication skills, both verbal and written. You'll never regret, on a personal or professional level, your improved ability to influence the world you live in.

Danita Bye

Talk to knowledgeable people about your concerns. It's your life. Ask lots of questions.

Anonymous

LEADERSHIP SKILLS

Be yourself. There is nothing more attractive than genuineness and authenticity.

Maggie Mortenson

The best business advice I ever got was that, in the long run, people hit only what they aim at. It is a bit corny, but I think true. I think that Thoreau said it first. The worst business's quote I ever heard was "ready, shoot, aim".... This was considered a truism during the dot-com boom. That didn't work out very well.

Barry Poltermann,
CEO Civilian Pictures

The best advice [I received] was provided by my father, who instilled in me qualities of high standards, high ethics, high morals, and offered me the advice that taking the high road would pay off most of the time, while trying to cut corners or cheat one's way through might pay off some of the time, but not often enough to make a difference.

Henry Stein

View all things as a learning opportunity. This will keep you fresh and open to innovative thinking. By striving to keep this as my mantra I am amazed at the opportunities that have been opened to me and the things I've learned along the way. It has also given me the confidence to share what I've learned with others.

Attitude is critical. A positive attitude allows you to be more likeable, approachable, and seems to be character strength in a leader during times of crisis.

One characteristic that I have observed in my own boss and many others that I have had the privilege to meet is "humbleness." There is no room for egos.

Marilyn Williams,
Executive Assistant to CEO, Best Buy Co., Inc.

Be an insatiable learner. You competition is getting better every day . . . you need to keep learning, stretching, and growing your own skills and beliefs. Commit to excellence in all that you do. Your work is your reputation.

Danita Bye

Many times life offers choices or opportunities that may look scary—because you might fail, because you might be laughed at, because it may turn out different than you think—but simply the opportunity itself will, no doubt, be a growing experience that will make you stronger and more self-confident. This is especially true as a young adult when so many opportunities present themselves in a variety of ways.

Maureen Fischer

Make a great plan. I believe that moving forward in life is what makes life interesting. Being afraid to try something new, not being challenged, waiting until you are forced to make a decision rather than making your own choices are things that make life boring...keep challenging yourself...find your own way.

Carol Rockler Chesen,
Edina Realty, Inc.

The biggest challenge for graduates is the difference in expectations from school to work (no excuses, no grades, etc.). The most important attribute is to show how you take responsibility and solve problems (rather than wait to be told, blame others, etc.)

Sherron Bienvenu, Ph.D.,
Professor Emerita, Emory University

The best advice I've received is from my former boss, Craig Palmer. He told me about the rule he uses called the "Three I's." You use this rule to help in decision making. The rule is "What you Initiate, think through all of the Implications and the Impact it may have in all directions." The Three I's are Initiate, Implications, and Impact.

Here's how it works. [Ask] exactly what do I want to initiate? (In one sentence, what is the crux of the idea?) Next, [ask] what are the implications? Lastly, if the idea is used, what are the ways it could impact others?

Debi Cain-Rivord,
TwinCities West Chapter of the International Association of Administrative
Professionals (IAAP)

SOCIAL SKILLS

People are the corporation or the school or the small business. The world of work is very diverse. Work is about more than just being smart and knowing the technical parts of your job—it is also about building relationships (one person at a time), connecting with others, and being respectful to [sic] any differences that may exist. Be "real"—everyone may not like you, but the people who do like you will like the real you.

Robbin Walker

Attend company functions, even if you have to attend alone. It is important to show you're supportive of any company event, if possible. You also will be enriched by meeting other people in your company.

Anonymous Office Manager

Get involved in company events, fund raising, etc. If the company is dedicated to raising money for the United Way, join a committee. Always talk with your manager/supervisor first to let them know your plans and assure them that this committee will not interfere with your job performance. This participation will enable you to do some good and your name will be known within the company as a team player. Ensure you follow through with anything you commit to.

Anonymous

My advice would be to treat others as you would like others to treat you, and have a mind-set for service.

Mark Neumann,
Comptroller, Essex Property Trust

Early on in my high school and college years I was taught by some very special role models that if you help enough other people succeed then you will indeed find potentially greater joy than if you focus on your own needs to the exclusion of others.

Steve Hall C.P.C.,
Senior Consultant, FGP International

My advice is to those who would love to live in a specific region of the country. Aim your job search very specifically at that area. It is much harder than you might think to move after you have held a job in another region for a period of time. You are invested in staying with that employer, you may marry someone from that region, your friends are there, and so on.

Suzanne Nelson

Treat everyone you meet with respect and honesty. You never know when or where your paths will cross again in this ever shrinking world. People are bridges to other people, opportunity, and success.

Karen Winner

I've learned not to prejudge people and situations. So many things are not what they seem . . . . Give things time...see more; meet more people; try more situations, both comfortable and uncomfortable. Be open to change because it's the only guaranteed situation you're going to find.

Anonymous

I've learned that as independent as I am, and like to be, I still need help from other people to achieve my goals...I need others to think highly of me, speak highly of me, and want to help me, which means I have to do my part first: To always give and speak well of others so that I can receive the same.

Peggy L. McNamara,
author of *My Tender Soul – A Story of Survival*

It's not what you know or how well you did in school—it's getting your foot in the door! The best way to do this is to use your existing network of friends, relatives, and acquaintances. Be shameless.

Be sure to send each one a thank you note and tell them how helpful they were and ask them to keep you in mind if they hear of anything. Then be sure to send them a note when you do get a job, and thank them again for their help. You will then have a large mentoring group in your own industry to call upon for advice and other referrals. Be sure to update them on your progress and send them all holiday cards. Also, ask them what groups you could join that would be helpful for the industry and for networking in general. Then join the groups and keep active.

Anonymous

Always keep your eyes and ears open through friends, family, and acquaintances. You never know who is looking for employee prospects...never write off previous friends/relationships—you never know when they will come back.

Nancy Shiff

Know that life's daily annoyances really aren't important. The most important elements in anyone's life, at any age, are family, friends, health, and happiness. The rest is "small stuff."

David Abramsage,
Writer, HGTV's "Designers' Challenge"

Work hard, but always remember that good relationships with those you value are more important than any paycheck! Good relationships, like anything worthwhile, take lots of hard work.

Anonymous

Become familiar with current events—read a national newspaper and a local paper. This should be done no less frequently than once each week, daily, if possible. Reading a current events magazine once in awhile is a good idea as well.

Anonymous

SELF-DISCIPLINE

Climbing the corporate ladder, making money, working long hours is no guarantee of personal happiness or measure of success. Finding the right balance between work and play is a key component to success and happiness...the scale of balance will shift depending on where you are in life. I think everyone should check in with himself or herself periodically and ask: Am I having fun? Am I focused at work or am I distracted? Where's my mind—here today, or thinking about the future?

If you're overworked and not taking time for yourself, distracted at work, and worrying about the future, it's time for re-alignment. Listen to the message your body is giving you.

Sandra D. Bullock,
Vice President, Institutional Sales

Be patient. Very seldom do you begin your career at peak. Develop an appreciation for what you learn and accomplish along the way to your goals.

Anonymous

Education counts! Getting an education is so important and will make a difference for the rest of one's life.

Anonymous

Find what you enjoy doing and build a career around it. Don't assume you already know by virtue of your major.

Rock Anderson,
Director of Recruiting Services and Diversity, Siemens Corporation

Follow your heart and your head. Years ago when I was younger, my motivation was money, promotion, status, etc. I was successful, but it felt empty. My heart urged me to pursue writing. My head told me to pursue financial success. Now, many years later, I know that I could have listened to my head and my heart and found a way to satisfy both. That's what I'm doing now and I'm very happy.

Wanda Craig,
W. B. Craig & Associates, Inc.

Keep a rolling account of your achievements, both at the workplace and outside (community, charity, work, etc.). Review your strengths and weaknesses objectively and identify what skills, beyond the obvious and [the] technical/functional, you used in a given situation. Examples of such skills might be persuasion, team motivation, leadership, conflict resolution.

Shefaly Yogendra,
Technology Policy and Strategy Consultant

Write down your goals. Some people do this in December; I like to do it around my birthday every year. I have goals in every area: personal, financial, spiritual, professional, etc. Think about what you want and focus on what's really important.

Danielle Voorhies,
Strategic Angle Marketing

If I could do anything differently, I would have followed my instinct and passion. It may have been difficult but I think I would have been happier with my career. I would have taken the risk instead of the safe way out.

Darlene Moss,
Career Development Coordinator, West Stanly High School

Follow your gut instinct. Sometimes when making a decision or hearing information, I turn it around in my head before acting on or absorbing it. However, sometimes I get an immediate "feeling"—a gut reaction—and I've learned that I should listen to it. If something seems "off," it probably is.

Keep learning. No matter what career you choose, most likely it is evolving all the time. To be successful, you need to actively pursue education and keep up to date with current trends.... Continuing education doesn't mean you need to continue going to college or take night classes. It can be as simple as attending a one-hour program once a month or a few-day program once or twice a year. Unless it's so expensive you can't afford it, sign up and consider it an investment in your future.

Debi Cain-Rivord

Focus on family and friends. They are the ones that will be there after you've been laid off, switched jobs, and struggled with bad bosses and companies. They will be your foundation and support during the inevitable changes in the business world.

Even when all you want to do is slam the alarm clock to stay in bed, knowing that your family and friends support you will help you peel away those warm protective sheets and deal with another day. Keep plugging away. Don't give up!

Michael Fisk,
Manager, New Media, MGM Studios

Trust the process. Being as impatient as I am, I tend to want things to happen right now, and the world doesn't always work that way. Trust the process simply means that if you go out every day and do the best you can with what you have, the results will show—eventually.

Anonymous

Your life is a sacred journey and path. Follow your vision with passion and take pride in the things of the heart which matter to you. Be unwilling to compromise your integrity. As you stand before it, at the end of each day, the mirror reflects your image's perspective. This reflection is the only one you must answer to.

Cary Brayboy,
Certified Personal Trainer,
Founder of Grey Wolf Fitness

As a new grad, remember, the most important step is to find that first job. Preferably in your field, but any job will get you into the world of work, and following a routine—getting up in the morning, learning the responsibility of being somewhere on time, putting in a full day of work, learning how to work with different people, etc. Also keep in mind that even if your first job is not your "dream" job or the job you want, to work hard, and learn as much as you can. Find a way to learn skills that can be used to get that next job up the ladder.

And if your salary is not what you want, remember, with experience comes better pay and better jobs. No matter what the profession, if you put the time, effort, and your all into it, the financial aspect of the career will eventually come.

Also, don't compare your job or your salary to your friends and other recent grads. People start out doing different things in different ways, and always remember it's not where you start, but where you finish.

Matt Krumrie,
Writer

I would encourage you to know who you are and what your values are and revisit those every time you need to make a major decision, whether it be personal or business.

Anonymous

Save money! When you get that first job you see an immediate rise in income. Start saving before you get used to spending the extra money. Maximize all 401K and employer matched retirement funds. If your employer matches, you save double.

Anonymous

Take 100 percent responsibility for yourself and your relationships. Too many people go through life with the attitude, "I am only 20 percent or 50 percent responsible for the success of this project or this relationship."

My dad used to say, "We create our own problems." Before I blame others, [I] first look in the mirror and ask myself, "What did I do or fail to do that may have caused this situation to occur?" There is a tremendous feeling of freedom when we are willing to accept responsibility for our actions or inactions.

Mike Norman,
President, Michael D. Norman & Associates

Believe in yourself—nobody knows you better than you....Listen to your heart. Do what you love, and you will do it well, and find a way to make money at it.

Anonymous

Look at the future and make choices based on your dreams. Finish your education while you are young and head for the big time.

Anonymous

The best advice I ever got was "Finish" from an author. He said there were many great writers in the world, but not many of them finish. Don't think that anything you choose is a life sentence. People change direction all the time and everything you do can help lead you to another exciting chapter in your life.

Wendy Baldinger,
Singer/Songwriter

The challenge for the graduate . . . is how to keep current and what to pay attention to. My "keep current" system is my rule of three. If I hear it, am exposed to it in any way three times, I check it out because something is going on. The "it" can be a book, a concept, [a] term, a company, a person. Whatever "it" is, I check it out.

My passionate commitment to being a lifelong learner and professional in my field is to read each day for one hour. . . . I heard that if you read for one hour a day in your field, in time you will be as knowledgeable as the perceived gurus in that field.

Beth Fischer

Go get some experience. Travel. Work at a non-profit or Starbuck's (where you will probably end up anyway for the next six months while you are searching). Get involved. Make a difference. Learn. Go to grad school (most definitely, go to grad school). Make mistakes. Have fun. Raise some Cain. You are still at an age where you can get away with it.

Don't be 40 years old with 15 or more years work experience and have nothing to show for it but a mortgage and a paunch. You will need those memories of good times as the work gets harder and the responsibilities such as marriage and kids come around.

There will always be time for work.

Rob Gelphman,
Principal, Gelphman Associates

If you have things in your life emotionally or physically that are stopping you from being the person you want to be, put considerable energy into working on those things. These may seem like personal issues, but they can dramatically impact your ability to make good business and career decisions, and they can impact your behavior on the job.

Beth Spencer

Don't let your age stop you from getting the education you want to change your life. Be willing to start at the bottom of your chosen profession.

Betty McMahon Buman

Don't think you're going to get your dream job immediately. It is going to take a lot of hard work, perseverance, and soul searching. Think with your head, but listen to your heart too.

Bonnie Blumenthal Stein

You're responsible for your own fiscal survival. This means that the majority of your activity from the minute you get out of bed until your work day ends is centered around making money. You have no control over your schedule whatsoever. You have to be in the office when your employer says you have to be, with little room for negotiation.

Anonymous

DEMONSTRATE A POSITIVE ATTITUDE

Stay open to different opportunities. It's okay not to plan every detail of the future. Sometimes you "fall" into opportunities that are better than anything you could have predicted or planned in advance.

Laurie Katz,
Director of Publicity, Facts On File, Inc.

I'd be less inhibited by fear. Fear will do you in every time. Don't be afraid to take risks, don't be afraid to stand alone, don't be afraid to ask questions, don't be afraid of rejection or failure. Everyone falls down; the people who are successful are the ones who get up and dust themselves off and keep going.

Try to excel no matter what you do—giving your all is very important, and people will recognize that you're a hard worker. But know that there is no shame in failing—the only shame is in not trying.

David Abramsage,
Writer, HGTV's "Designers' Challenge"

The only person you can really control in your life is yourself. Therefore, learn to really like yourself—put a lot into your life so you will be comfortable with who you are.

Leslie,
Interior Designer

A recent graduate may feel intimidated or insecure due to lack of experience. I would suggest they act confidently, even if they're not. I would also recommend talking to someone who has done what they want to do. We can all learn from someone else's experience. Whether they are going to further their education or look for a job, the world is a scary place and you have to be competitive. Look people in the eye, give them a firm handshake, and sell yourself. Look for opportunities and make it happen.

Anonymous

Money isn't everything. Family, friends, and loved ones will ultimately make you happy.

Walter Keen Wilkins,
Research Manager, Earthlink, Inc.

The best advice I ever got was from my dad. He told me that if I worked hard, treated people with respect, and always did my best, that I could have any career that I wanted. He suggested that I find out what made me unique as that uniqueness would make me stand out from the other grads. He said that I was the only one who could limit my dreams.

Carol Fredrickson,
Violence Free

Figure out what your unique abilities are. I think too many people choose careers for the wrong reason. . . . I think when people are doing what they love and are inherently good at, work doesn't become a burden.

Anonymous

Be true to yourself, be honest, have balance in your life, always maintain a sense of humor, listen, and treat others as you would expect to be treated.

Beth Sterling,
VP Sales, BizRate.com

Follow your heart, dream big, and be persistent. If you get knocked down, dust off the dirt and strap your shoes on better. Look at everything as an experience and a stepping stone to the next level. There truly is no bad experience—it's all good learning. And the learning should never stop. Risks are something you need to take to get to where you want to go. Just look before you leap.

Holly Jo Anderson,
Veritas Marketing, LLC

Realize that the company will hire you only if it is to their benefit and not to yours. Remember, the purpose of Human Resources is to screen you out. They do not hire you; they just keep you from being hired.

Ernie Simpson,
President, Wizardco International, Inc.

Some voices are more equal than others . . . expect to have a voice, expect to offer an opinion, and at the same time, don't expect to have everything go your way. Cream rises to the top . . . don't ever feel you are too good to do anything you are assigned. It isn't the task you're completing that establishes your worth; it's your attitude. Be positive, and you'll rise to the top.

Anonymous

AREAS OF DISTINCTION

Everyone is on his or her own timetable, his own journey, and that success is defined by oneself, not by peers or the media or society. The path that you take to success is right for you. It might not be the path traveled by everyone else, and that's okay. And sometimes the road less taken is indeed the most interesting path of all.

David Abramsage,
Writer, HGTV's "Designers' Challenge"

Learn how money works first. Learn how and how much to save, how to protect yourself, and how to take advantage of different tax structures legitimately.

Usah Christi

It would be wise . . . to talk with someone working in his/her chosen field of employment and residence to become at least slightly more conscious of current practices, trends in practice and ways of life, including local politics, where the person plans to live.

Anonymous

Fresh out of high school I loved music and cars. Without a real vehicle for music I went with the auto industry. Years later I was camping in a remote island with no power, no phones—nothing. But I had a cell phone and pager so BMW could reach me on vacation. When I returned home I handed in my resignation and went to audio school. Twelve months later I was hired by a firm in Dallas and sent out on a Rolling Stones tour. Since then I've been around the world with multiple national recording artists, and although the money is not quite as much as before and the work is grueling at times, it was the best move I've ever made. I have no regrets. Find your passion.

Mical Caterina

Get involved. Make a commitment to keep learning and growing as an individual. Get involved in industry associations. Spend time with people you admire or people who have done what you strive to do. The fact is we're all going to change careers several times, and when you find a new job, it is usually the result of knowing someone, not answering an ad in the paper.

Danielle Voorhies
Strategic Angle Marketing

You can find your biggest victories in your worst defeats. Failure allows you to see what type of people you need to surround yourself with to succeed. And, ultimately in failure you have an end point. Many people pass through their lives being just okay. They never stop to think about what could be because they are comfortable. Failure is not comfortable; it forces you to change directions. If you play it safe, you will lead an average existence.

Stephanie Ratko,
Marketing Communications, FinancialAid.com

Always assume that your employer will never give you enough training, and much of what you learn will be "on the job" training. Also, assume that someone at work will be angry with you for not knowing what no one ever taught you. That's life.

Mistakes will be often forgiven, if you disclose them early enough. Rare is the mistake that can't be corrected, if you disclose it early enough.

The contemplation of an act is worse than its execution.

When it feels like the world is closing in on you, take time to do something mildly irresponsible. Go for a walk. Shut the door and take a catnap. Refuse to accept incoming calls.

Anonymous

Be prepared—never assume anything and be ready for everything. Good thought, but difficult to do!

Realize that you don't know everything. Find an older person to bounce ideas off of and listen, listen, listen to what they have to say.

Learn how to give to others—by helping others, volunteering, sharing what you have, mission trips to third world countries, etc. By giving, you receive much more in return than you ever gave.

I would expand my horizons a bit more, try new things more quickly, and not take myself so seriously at times. I would laugh more.

It is essential to help young people to recognize their strengths and help them utilize them. Not to settle, but excel. To hold out for what they want, and believe in achieving it.

Anonymous

Pay most attention to corporate culture. How you are treated will mean the most in whether you like your job.

Sherron Bienvenu, Ph.D.,
Professor Emerita, Emory University

Although I have been very blessed with my career, I believe pursuing a college degree would have been beneficial. I was married right out of high school and had to wait for my husband to finish college before we could afford for me to go. After four years of waiting, I was ready to settle down and college was the furthest thing from my mind. I wish I had pursued my passion of having a degree in business. Although my years of experience has helped me achieve my goals, I believe a college education would have given me more opportunities.

Anonymous Entrepreneur

I learned as a senior in high school that believing in something greater than yourself was the key to living in this world.

Steve Hall C.P.C.,
Senior Consultant, FGP International

I think the very most important thing to search for when choosing a career is to find something that you can enjoy doing, and then put all of your energy into it. If you can, at the end of the day, honestly say that you'd do whatever it is that you were doing for free as if you didn't need the money, then you have truly hit the jackpot.

Barry Witkow,
Vice President, Software Solutions, eSpeed, Inc.

JAN   2007

DATE DUE
